PRAISE F(

Get Past Your Past

You might feel that moving beyond your pain and heartache is insurmountable, but you're never alone. Jason VanRuler will truly help you get past your past for good with this book. Let the wisdom in these pages move you toward a brighter, more courageous, and well-connected future.

—Jon Acuff, *New York Times* bestselling author,
Soundtracks: The Surprising Solution to Overthinking

Healing from our past is often something we say we want, but is often hard to do. We have the desire, but not the know-how. Jason VanRuler brilliantly gives us powerful tools and insights from his own lived experiences to get us there. It is filled with nuggets of gold that will help you flourish and thrive. I absolutely love this book!

—Mike Foster, executive counselor;
author, *The Seven Primal Questions*

This timely treasure-trove from Jason VanRuler is packed with biblical wisdom, clinical insights, practical solutions, and personal triumphs that will help *you* overcome life's hardships, embrace healing, and progress toward meaningful connections. Let me break it down into five words: boom sauce for the soul!

—Chuck E. Tate, pastor;
author; podcaster

It's rare for anyone to make it through life unscathed. If Hurt and Healing are archenemies, then Hurt knows how to reach us all and Healing seems to be only an urban legend. This book proves that healing is real. Not only is it real, it's obtainable. I'm grateful to know Jason VanRuler and to learn from him. Do your soul a favor and get your hands on this book.

—Chris Durso, author,
The Heist: How Grace Robs Us of Our Shame

There are so many things I love about my dear friend Jason. He's one of the most approachable people I've ever met. He's so kind, yet willing to say the hard thing. He's witty (and self-deprecating). He loves God. He has vast knowledge and experience as a therapist. In these pages, I have no doubt his insight will help you get past your past. This book will meet you right where you are, while at the same time challenging you not to stay there.

—Adam Weber, lead pastor, Embrace Church; author;
host, *The Conversation* podcast

Jason VanRuler, a great dude and an awesome therapist who has a lot of those abbreviations after his name, wrote a book called *Get Past Your Past* where he challenges you to confront your past hurts, helps you move through them, and provides encouragement and a legit friend for the journey every step of the way. Also, I've been thinking, why is abbreviation such a long word?

—Michael Jr., comedic thought-leader; author,
Funny How Life Works

In *Get Past Your Past*, Jason VanRuler takes us on a journey from greater self-awareness to deeper healing. Most people know Jason as a successful counselor, executive coach, or podcaster. As a personal friend (and fellow South Dakotan), I know Jason as someone who is very intentionally compassionate in the way he listens to and cares for those around him.

—Cade Thompson, artist;
songwriter; worship leader

Jason VanRuler provides a comforting acknowledgment that to some degree or another, we are all broken. You may have never considered the burdensome quote-posters you have hanging on the walls of your heart, but through stories from his own healing journey, Jason illuminates them and prods us to move toward health, healing, and wholeness. With clinical insights, relevant biblical examples, and relationship wisdom, Jason guides us along a path toward community and connection. *Get Past Your Past* is the guidebook you need to finally get past your own past.

—Dr. Zoe M. Shaw, author;
psychotherapist

GET
PAST
YOUR
PAST

GET PAST YOUR PAST

How Facing Your Broken Places
Leads to True Connection

Jason VanRuler

ZONDERVAN BOOKS

ZONDERVAN BOOKS

Get Past Your Past
Copyright © 2023 by Solomon Recovery

Requests for information should be addressed to:
Zondervan, *3900 Sparks Dr. SE, Grand Rapids, Michigan 49546*

Zondervan titles may be purchased in bulk for educational, business, fundraising, or sales promotional use. For information, please email SpecialMarkets@Zondervan.com.

ISBN 978-0-310-36743-7 (audio)

Library of Congress Cataloging-in-Publication Data

Names: VanRuler, Jason, 1980– author.
Title: Get past your past : how facing your broken places leads to true connection / Jason VanRuler.
Description: Grand Rapids : Zondervan, 2023.
Identifiers: LCCN 2023026110 (print) | LCCN 2023026111 (ebook) | ISBN 9780310367413 (trade paperback) | ISBN 9780310367420 (ebook)
Subjects: LCSH: Suffering—Religious aspects—Christianity. | Pain—Religious aspects—Christianity. | Addicts—Religious life. | BISAC: RELIGION / Christian Living / Family & Relationships | PSYCHOLOGY / Mental Health
Classification: LCC BV4909 .V365 2023 (print) | LCC BV4909 (ebook) | DDC 248.8/6 —dc23/eng/20230717
LC record available at https://lccn.loc.gov/2023026110
LC ebook record available at https://lccn.loc.gov/2023026111

The author is represented by Tom Dean, literary agent with A Drop of Ink LLC, www .adropofink.pub.

Cover design: Curt Diepenhorst
Cover illustration: TMvectorart / Shutterstock
Interior design: Kait Lamphere

Printed in the United States of America
23 24 25 26 27 LBC 5 4 3 2 1

This book is dedicated to my brilliant wife, Jodi, and our three children.

Jodi, even though your business suit was just a phase, your love wasn't. Thank you for seeing me and loving me and for all the grace along the way.

Thank you to J. Oliver, Isla, and Finnegan: you have taught me as much as I could ever hope to teach each of you about life and love. I will always be your biggest cheerleader and proud father.

I also dedicate this book to my friend Bob Goff, who encouraged me to love others, be bold, and dream big. Thank you for teaching me to write, for fielding my frequent questions, and for being a mentor.

To everyone that has long felt or believed that they were too broken, wounded, or injured to have meaningful connection, this book is for you. My hope is that you will see yourself as God sees you and let others see that beautiful light. The world has been waiting for you, and I can't wait for you to get connected.

CONTENTS

PART 3:
Embracing Your Connection

FOREWORD

I've been good friends with Jason for a while now, and I know he was meant to write this book. Jason would be the first to tell you he hasn't always been the person he is today. Like most of us, he has walked through some really hard stuff in his past, but he's used that brokenness and hurt to meet people where they are and help them become whole again.

In *Get Past Your Past*, Jason shares stories and struggles that paint a picture of a man who took circumstances he could have used as an excuse to become bitter and jaded and instead turned them into his testimony. He has taken what he's experienced personally and professionally as a talented clinician and distilled those experiences into a message we can all relate to. He shows us how to move past our past by leading us along a path that ends in connection, no matter how broken we may feel. I know that what he writes about will hit home for you, just like it did for me.

We were all made for love and connection. Don't let your brokenness get in the way of that promise.

—Bob Goff, *New York Times* bestselling author

PREFACE

I remember it like it was yesterday.

The first time I realized I was completely broken, I'd just woken up from a terrible night of drinking and using drugs. Disheveled, sick, and with an empty wallet, I was in an apartment I couldn't afford, hours from anywhere I'd known growing up, and had nothing but an unstable job and lots of debt.

I looked in the mirror and didn't like the person who looked back. *Loathed* would not be too strong a word. I grew up with lots of trauma and woundedness, and I remembered being that little boy who promised himself he'd run away from anything even close to the abuse, addiction, chaos, and conflict he was witnessing and suffering. And yet here I was, in many ways acting out the same patterns I had seen as a kid, often with the same results.

During this season, sitting in that apartment all alone, I was sure my life was pretty much over and would never get any better. And yet it did. My first step was to own where I was and ask for help. My life wasn't how I had dreamed, planned, or hoped it to be, but I admitted how it actually was. Gradually I looked in the mirror not with disgust but with the resolve of someone who is prepared to take on a project that requires a lot of work. I didn't have awareness or a plan like I do today. I just wanted to feel better and to move on from the pain and exhaustion I felt. Maybe you've felt this way before? Exhausted and struggling, but ready to make a change.

I'd like to say I changed immediately after that day, but I didn't. Instead, my life was a chaotic dance, going back and forth between brokenness and healing for the next couple of years. I experienced less brokenness, but that shattered person I saw in the mirror was never far away.

Along the way I picked lots of fights with God. I blamed, screamed, pleaded, and just about everything else I could think of. After a while I even swore God off. I think it was when I attempted to install the fourteenth metal rivet on a trailer at my job working for a trailer manufacturing company that I wouldn't keep past the first day. As the rivet bent and the metal twisted, I looked around the exceedingly hot rectangle of metal I was sitting in with ten other guys who worked there, all of us sweating, sparks flying, and I gave up on God.

It just seemed so much easier than trying to figure it out. What's weird is that I half expected God to rip open the trailer in some sort of cinematic effort to find his now very lost sheep, but that's not what happened. Instead, a spark flew into my shirt and I flailed around like a kid who has been stung by a bee, and the guy next to me smiled and said, "You'll get used to getting burned a couple times a day, man."

I won't spoil the story, but God and I reconciled not long after that day when I finally slowed down enough to feel everything that I had been running from for so many years. It was in that moment of silence that I saw the truth, which was that I had never really been alone.

Eventually, with the help of some friends and a therapist, I addressed the wounds from my past that had been pulling the strings all along. I learned that some of the problems I was facing weren't new ones but old ones in disguise, kind of like the bad guy in every *Scooby Doo* mystery. I developed a different relationship with alcohol and stopped using drugs. I acknowledged the pain that I had both endured and caused in my brokenness. I started to hear the whisper of God's voice. Not often, but it was more than it had ever been. Things were far from perfect, but there was the slightest bit of change happening. There was hope.

After I became a therapist, I was sure I would find out that I was doing everything wrong, that someone would point out a fatal flaw in my strategy, an Achilles' heel, or a red flag I'd missed and the bottom would fall out.

And so I kept working, learning, and growing. I took all the courses, attended the seminars, sat in circles, journaled, and meditated like it was going out of style.

I founded two private practices where I worked with clients from all walks of life. There were days when I'd see someone who was freshly out of prison, followed by a wealthy businessperson, and nearly every time, it was a version of the same thing: people felt broken in some way by past hurts, wounds, or trauma, and it led them to feel disconnected from those around them. In this disconnection, they felt alone, unseen, and stuck.

So I taught them the plan that I had used to deal with my past and build a life that I could have only dreamed of as a kid.

I knew that I was onto something when I watched lives change and clients overcome their pasts and get connected.

Even though my plan was working for others, I waited a long time to share it for fear of rejection.

Years later, that changed. I found some good friends, got a mentor, and had a transformative experience at a retreat. I was still full of doubt that anyone would want to hear the plan, but I could no longer ignore the encouragement of family, friends, and God.

So I took a step out and started a social media account thinking that nothing would happen. But seemingly overnight I had a hundred thousand followers and I knew it was time.

I spent so many years letting things that had happened in the past make me feel broken and run the show, and I know it's not easy to shine a light on those places. But if you are willing, I'd be honored to help you take the things you think make you broken, defective, and unlovable and transform them into meaningful connection.

Join me as we examine the answers to these questions and more:

- Why is it so difficult to move beyond our past?
- How do we change our relationship to the past so that it empowers us instead of holds us back?
- What lessons can we learn about the past that can help us today?
- How do we turn the past into a superpower that connects us with others?

Preface

I wrote this book for everyone, not only as a guide as they navigate these stages but also as a reference for the times when they feel stuck and alone. I needed to write it to get a firmer grip on what truly mattered to get me to the life I now live. I don't know that my story is all that special or that what I've accomplished is unusual or exemplary. I don't have it all figured out, but I have found a few ideas about how to get where you really want to go. At the very least, I want you to know that you are not alone in your journey or the exception to the rule. In the stories to follow, I'll share some of the pitfalls I've endured and the lessons I've learned along the way, which are rooted in psychology, biblical wisdom, and my clinical experience as a therapist. From them, I hope you'll find that it's not so farfetched to believe you can once and for all establish the mindset of emotional health and resilience, and know that you have what it takes to practice it. So many others are in the same place with similar goals as you, and I believe the life you dream of isn't so far away.

If you're ready to address your past and want to learn to better embrace love and connection, I hope you'll join me and the many others who are seeking this timeless and timely wisdom together.

The past is our definition. We may strive
with good reason to escape it, or to escape
what is bad in it. But we will escape it
only by adding something better to it.

—*Wendell Berry,*
"The Specialization of Poetry"

PART 1

REDISCOVERING
YOUR CONTROL

To wrestle with our past is to wrestle with control—feeling like we've lost it, given it up, or never had it to begin with. Because it feels terrible to wrestle with control and the uncertainty that comes with it, we usually react in one of two ways: relinquish control or become rigid and controlling.

While these responses are understandable, neither is ideal because both require us to abandon ourselves. And when we abandon ourselves, we trade authenticity and vulnerability for isolation and unhappiness. While this seems like a fair trade in the moment, over time isolation and unhappiness become increasingly difficult to maintain and eventually lead us back to where we started, like we're on a merry-go-round of pain that we can't get off.

This section of the book will show you how to stop wrestling, get off the merry-go-round, and see that you've been holding the key to your future the whole time.

Chapter 1

LETTING IT OUT

Our past shapes us in profound ways whether we admit it or not. Although we may be ruthlessly committed to facing forward in our present life, our past powers our future and the decisions we make today, whether consciously or subconsciously. For some, this revelation is like a springboard into a wonderful life, but for others of us, it's like shackles chained to our ankles, which we must drag with us forever. And so we do. We do our best to hope for better while hearing the clunk, clunk, clunk with every step we take. It's exhausting and uncomfortable, and worse, it's not sustainable. Shackles prevent us from running and instead slow us down to a walk or even a shuffle. We usually start off strong as young adults, but over time life becomes an endurance race, and we eventually wind up with wobbly legs and find ourselves overcome with pain, crawling slowly to the finish line of our life.

Maybe that's where this book finds you today, watching others run past, while you are left wondering where things went wrong and how you might get up again. I've been there, and I see you. It's a miserable spot to be in because when you're lying on the ground, everything looks better than where you are. From that position it can be easy to wonder:

- What is wrong with me?
- Why does everything have to be so difficult?
- Can life get better?
- Where is God in all of this?

While all of these are painful things to wonder, the one that is by far the worst is this: Should I just learn to expect that this is my life and quit trying?

This question is the one that gets people, because answering yes means that they've accepted the pain. Although giving up feels better in the moment, it costs you your potential and ensures that the bad things that have happened to you are no longer pauses along the timeline of your life but full stops.

Here's the good news, though: there is a way to get back up and it's different from what you think. It doesn't require a time machine, denial, or living in a fantasy, but it does require being honest with yourself and facing where you have come from.

Aristotle said, "Give me a child until he is seven and I will show you the man." But what if that isn't true? What if you could take a messy, hurtful, broken, or undesirable past and use it to build something beautiful? It seems hard to believe, but people do it every day. Countless people have taken challenging, difficult, or even nearly impossible circumstances and used them to fuel a new life. And when they do, it makes quite a story.

The thing is that no one really ever talks about how it's

done. We all agree that bad things happen and that many of us feel wounded, broken, or dismayed when considering the past, but not many people offer guidance of how to get past it. Because sometimes the people who seemingly get past it actually don't. They just develop stronger ankles, carry the shackles more efficiently, or even get someone else to help carry them, but the shackles are still there. And although these responses buy them some time, they still have to face their past if they ever want to move freely into a new life.

Getting past your past isn't an obligation, it's an invitation. And like all invitations, there are some directions. The first one is to cough.

After COVID, almost everyone has had the experience of wearing a mask at the grocery store, at work, or worst of all, at church and feeling a terrible urge to cough. You know you aren't sick, but coughing is going to make everyone near you think you are, so you hold it back. As you do, tears stream down your face and you try one of those semicough, throat-clearing things, but it doesn't work. And in a few seconds, you're going to have to let out this huge cough and risk becoming completely socially unacceptable.

It's a terrible feeling, but a lot of us go through our lives this way trying not to let out our true feelings. I know because I've been there. Things happen and we need to address them or say how they've affected us, but instead we avoid the reality and the conversations and do as little as possible to make it through, hoping it'll go away. And maybe sometimes it works. But if it doesn't, we end up making a scene or just create more problems for ourselves. And some feelings just won't be swallowed. They have to come out.

When I work with clients, one of the biggest honors is sitting with someone when they "cough" for the first time. It's often such a powerful moment when I get to watch someone come back to life. It's painful too, because I know how long they've held that cough and simply learned to deal with the symptoms.

I remember the first time I "coughed" after holding it in for a very long time. It was after that terrible night I described in the preface to this book, when I looked at myself in the mirror with self-loathing and decided I wanted to move on from my pain and exhaustion.

Though I was sure my life would never get better, gradually it did.

One day at work a beautiful woman walked in to talk to my colleague. My heart lit up when I saw her in her fancy business suit. I was smitten. We dated and things moved quickly toward marriage. I knew I had to address my brokenness to keep the relationship and I had no idea what I was doing, but I wanted so desperately to be chosen by this woman. We recognized that there would be challenges ahead but decided to marry and start a life together. Jodi showed me grace, and for what felt like the first time in my life, I was truly loved.

Love changed my heart, but not my habits. I struggled to receive Jodi's love and often complicated things by acting out negative patterns and behavior that I had yet to address. I wanted so badly to be loved but was more terrified than ever because now I had something to lose. I could be rejected and thrown to the side, and the fear of loss outweighed everything else.

Those first years of marriage were rough, like being a pioneer in a desolate land hoping to have a few days without a blizzard. What pushed everything forward was the idea that life could be different, even though a lot of days that hope seemed distant. Over time, I came to believe I could be loved for who I was and to accept the love that Jodi and those around me were giving me. My heart softened and things changed.

Initially, love was like a shirt your mother buys a little too large for you so you can grow into it. It fit in some places, but I struggled to fill it out. I spent lots of time working on accepting love and loving others, and even though there were some significant hardships and I missed the mark a lot, I made progress toward becoming a person who wholeheartedly believes in the importance of loving and being loved.

This is the part where people usually get stuck. They cough once, they do some work, life improves, and they settle into complacency. But life is a series of coughs, and as much as we'd like to think otherwise, more coughs will come.

The second cough caught me wildly off guard, like when someone shouts "Heads up!" at a baseball game but the ball is already about to hit you. Although several things had to happen before it hit you, you just don't really expect it. And in some ways, getting hit when you don't expect it hurts the worst.

Despite our marriage improving, Jodi and I struggled to have children. Struggled is probably being a little too positive. Struggled as in had several miscarriages and an ectopic pregnancy after which we were told that we could no longer have biological children.

Hurting but persistent, we decided to pursue adoption. We made an adoption book, did the home study, and were even considered by some birth mothers. It was a difficult time in our lives, but we tried to be optimistic.

Eventually we received a call about an opportunity that seemed like it was going to work. We talked a bit with the birth mother and it seemed like we were on the same page. We were elated.

Over the next months, we did everything new parents are supposed to do. We bought the car seat, designed the nursery, bought ridiculously expensive swaddling blankets, and the whole works. We were as invested as we could be and could hardly wait for the opportunity to drive across several states to meet the birth mother and our child.

But it never happened. When we arrived at the hospital after the child had been born, we learned that the birth mother had changed her mind. It was her decision to make, and although I understood it, we were wrecked.

After sitting at the hospital for a couple of hours, we drove home, but there was such a heaviness in the car. We'd lost a child—again. I just remember driving mile after mile, passing cornfield after cornfield, and feeling stuck in my pain. I didn't know what I could possibly say to Jodi, who, more than anything, wanted a child and had already been through so much with the surgeries and miscarriages. Now this hopeful possibility had been taken away. What do you say to someone in this situation? I just didn't know.

As we drove silently through Nebraska, I put on a song by the Avett Brothers, "I and Love and You." I'm not sure what the band was thinking about when they wrote it, but the sentiment of it is, I'm in rough shape. I'm feeling bad and I need to be taken care of. It's a song we both liked, but it's arguably a sad song.

For the first time in my life, I coughed with someone else—my second cough. I didn't know it then, but today I recognize that seeing I wasn't alone in my pain was life changing. Together we coughed our dashed dream, our feelings of anger and sadness, our uncertainty about the future.

I listened to the song and cried. When it was finished, I put it on repeat. I sang and cried, and Jodi cried too. We found that if we could share that song, we could share that moment. I'm not going to lie by saying the rest of the drive was okay. It was terrible, one of the worst trips I've ever made. But each time we listened to that song, we connected. We connected over our shared grief. We connected over our not knowing what to say or how to comfort each other. We connected over our inability to put a positive spin on what had just happened, but knowing that life would go on.

I'll never forget that somber drive up the driveway to our house and sitting in the garage with that empty carseat in the back. We had done everything we were supposed to do, prayed about it, had the right intentions, gave it our all, and yet here we were, with an empty nursery and a broken dream. It wasn't supposed to be like this. Clunk, clunk, clunk went the shackles as I got out of the car and shuffled into the silent house.

I realized that day that getting past your past is less like having a root canal and more like brushing your teeth. You have to get good at dealing with the daily gunk. Some days will be messier than others. Some messes will be huge and earth shattering, while others will be small and add up over time, but the routine stays the same.

Accepting the invitation to get past your past isn't about changing your past, it's about changing your mind.

Take a moment to write down the times that you have "coughed." Who was there when it happened? What was the outcome? What experiences, issues, or wounds have you been avoiding that you need to address?

Chapter 2

YOU'RE NOT AS BROKEN AS YOU THINK

What if the things you believe about yourself aren't completely true?

What if you're more than what you've been labeled?

What if that thing you did in the past doesn't define your future?

We're all broken people; that's just reality. We all will mess up, do things we regret, and fail. We all have parts of ourselves, our histories, our behaviors, and our experiences that make us feel broken, but are we as broken as we think?

My friend Sam had a difficult childhood. Although he believed that his parents loved him, they struggled to show him that love and instead were often abusive. Amid the abuse, Sam's young years were rife with chaos, problems, and hardship.

As if that weren't enough, at a young age Sam was informed he was terribly allergic to peanuts. Being a kid with a serious nut allergy is like having an exhausting part-time job where you could die if you make a mistake. You must always watch not only what you eat but what everyone around you eats. Slip up and the consequences can be severe. So along with all the other stress and chaos in his childhood, Sam had this deadly peanut allergy that came to define his life.

Until one day in college. Sam forgot to check for peanuts and drank a protein shake that was full of peanut-butter powder. When he realized what he had just drunk, Sam rushed to the hospital, certain he was a goner.

But the people at the hospital told Sam he was fine. A bit confused, the doctor had done some tests and found out Sam wasn't allergic to peanuts after all. Now, of course, Sam was elated. But that elation soon turned to confusion and anger when he realized what it meant. He called his mom and asked why his parents had always told him he had a peanut allergy. Apparently when he was a kid it had been suggested by a doctor that Sam *might* be allergic to peanuts, but his parents had never confirmed it. Sam wasn't deathly allergic (or allergic at all!) to peanuts like he thought he was.

Now, you might think this is a story about hating your parents, but it's not. Although Sam was angry, he later forgave his parents. But more important than that, in one day Sam learned that something he had believed about himself for his entire life was inaccurate. He had expended so much mental energy avoiding a danger that wasn't really there. He'd missed so many chances to eat Reese's Peanut Butter Cups and peanut-butter and jelly sandwiches, all because of a faulty belief. (This is probably a good time to mention that allergies are nothing to mess around with. If you question the validity of a diagnosis, get a second opinion, okay?)

What I've learned working with counseling clients and going through my own therapy is that sometimes truths we firmly believe about ourselves aren't true. Sometimes "the way it is" isn't the way it is. Being aware that these truths—whether they were told to us by someone else or we told ourselves—might not be true is often the key to making changes and gaining confidence.

I cannot tell you how beautiful it is to see a group of clients I'm working with bare their deepest souls to each other and, in honest conversation, learn that they don't seem as bad or broken or messed up to each other as they do to themselves. These individuals are so sure their experiences confirm that they're bad or terrible people, that a part of them is broken because of something that was said or done to them or that they did in the past. But no one else in the room sees them that way. That's just how they see themselves.

Early on in my career while I was going to graduate school to become a therapist, I worked as a real-estate appraiser for my wife's real-estate company. It made sense for us to work together, so I pursued a licensure and began joining her on appraisal inspections.

One day after measuring a house, we returned to the office, where Jodi reviewed my measurements. They were way off. Thankfully, Jodi is a stickler for detail, so we went back to the house and she asked me to show her how I measured it. I puffed out my chest and showed her how to measure a house correctly.

A smile spread across her face.

"What?" I asked.

Jodi showed me that there are two sides to the measuring tape. I had used the wrong side, marked in centimeters rather than inches.

Even though I had measured the whole house and seemingly done everything correctly, the results were, well, wrong. I had used the wrong side of the tape measure, so all my measurements were off. The answer I was so sure about wasn't actually right.

I wonder how often we do this in our lives. How often do we measure ourselves with a tape measure that is no longer, or never even was, accurate for our needs? We're at the right house, going through all the right motions, but using the wrong measure, and all the results are skewed.

In such a case, we need a Jodi. Someone else, someone who knows the truth about who we are, who is able to carefully and specifically tell us why our way of measuring ourselves isn't accurate. We need to be able to respect and trust the person telling us these truths. We need to be certain they have our best interests at heart. When someone cares enough to tell us the truth about ourselves, we need to be willing to turn over the tape measure, then to measure again. We need to look at changing what we believe about ourselves. Although this doesn't sound difficult, it's rarely easy to open ourselves up to a new way of thinking about and talking to ourselves.

Although it's tough to flip over the tape, when our friends help us see that we are better than we've measured ourselves, we build confidence and form deeper relationships. Believe it or not, the best relationships aren't the ones where you're told to simply carry on as you've been doing. The best relationships are the ones where people are willing to tell you the truth regardless of how it might make you feel.

When we find relationships like this, our world gets bigger and brighter, not just because we see ourselves in a new light but also because we see others with the same objectivity and grace.

Jodi and I try to keep to a minimum the number of quote pictures and signs with sayings on them in our house. (There are only so many times you can be reminded to "live, laugh, love.") But we do have one that a friend gave us, which says, "As for me and my house, we will serve the Lord," and every time I see that saying framed on the wall, I think of the person who gave it to us. I love that personal connection.

I think sometimes we're given a mental version of one of those quote pictures, one with a belief about ourselves printed on it. Maybe it's a belief someone else has about us, or maybe it's one we gave ourselves, but we just tack that quote up on the wall of our hearts and never think much about whether it's true, because after all, it looks official or something, right? If someone gave it to us, it must be true. Right?

Right?

Well, not necessarily. After all, sometimes we were raised by people who were not very healthy or who had limited awareness of and insight about who we are. Or maybe our friends weren't really friends. Or maybe there are any of a million reasons that someone gave us one of those boards that says something totally wrong. Something like "You're the only one going through this" or "You're terrible" or "You're never going to change," and now, having spent years allowing our experiences to reinforce this belief, we are convinced it must be true. We simply never really think about it. We never take that picture down off the wall of our hearts. Sure, it's not as nice as one of those Joanna Gaines quote pictures they sell for like $50 at Target, but we keep it up in our hearts like it is. We look at it all the time. We learn to take it for granted. *That's just how it is.* We never stop to think about whether it's true.

But what if we did stop to think? What if we were willing to go over the walls of our hearts and examine the things we believe about ourselves? What if we found the courage to say, *This isn't actually that helpful to me anymore. I think I need to take that down.* Jesus did this when he challenged a tax collector named Matthew to see himself in a new light. Could the truth about ourselves be different from what we hung on our walls all those years ago?

We want to live in a world where everything is the way we perceive it to be. Our brains are trying to help us by establishing this sense of "these are the rules and the structures in which we live." Because they're already making so many decisions every single day, it just makes things easier for them if there's an established order, if they can partition off that this or that is true about us.

If I decide that I'm a bad person who does bad things, then I don't have to think about what it would be like if I weren't a bad person. It's time saving for our brains to operate this way, but it also might be keeping us stuck in misery by forcing us onto a path that no longer takes us to our desired destination. The truth is harder. It's also better. Much better.

Take a moment. Think about the quote pictures you have hanging in your heart. What's on them? Get specific. Be honest. Let yourself be uncomfortable for a moment and try to be objective. Are the messages true? Are they false? Or did they used to be true but aren't any longer? Might it be time to take the signs down? Might it be time to rephrase them? Time to eliminate them altogether? It's worth examining the truths you're believing and making decisions about them. If you're going to believe something negative about yourself, then it's mandatory that you trace the origin of that belief and show proof that it's true.

The key here is simply the willingness to examine our beliefs about ourselves. You might conclude that the belief is true or that it might just be slightly different, but at least consider questioning it and talking to other people about that belief. What you'll find is that we all have these things hanging in our hearts, and we rarely talk about them. But if we'll talk about them, we'll often find that someone else believes something similar about themselves too, and we're not alone. Maybe it's time for them to make a change too. Or maybe they've dealt with that belief in a healthier way than how we're dealing with it, but we'll never know if we don't talk about it. The challenge here is identifying the pictures you have hanging up in your heart and choosing to keep them up or take them down. I know that my life changed dramatically when I took down the sign that said "Jason's childhood ruined him" and replaced it with something more accurate.

Every so often it's important to look at the things we tell ourselves about who we are and figure out where these beliefs came from and if we want to continue to believe them. Sometimes we're right and the way we see ourselves is accurate. Other times, we are wrong.

Here's a secret that my experience has taught me: you're probably not as broken as you think.

Take a moment to write down your negative and limiting beliefs about yourself. Are you using the right side of the tape measure? If you aren't sure, talk with a trusted friend to see what comes up.

Chapter 3

YOUR PAST DOESN'T CHANGE YOUR VALUE

My first car was a 1984 Chevy Citation. For those who don't know, this car is the equivalent of a Gremlin, or if you're still too young to know what *that* is, a really old Honda Civic. The point is, my first car was not one many people dream of owning.

What's more, I purchased my Chevy Citation from a man whose wife drove it and apparently struggled to appreciate colors other than electric blue and maroon. Hence my electric blue Chevy Citation with a maroon interior. While it did a great job of getting me around, it was not the type of car I would put much effort into improving. While I watched my friends save for new stereos or rims for their rides, I simply saved for a whole different car. I was so sure my Chevy Citation was too ugly and broken to improve that I did nothing to fix it or make it better—or even maintain it. When a hubcap fell off, I just left it, and when a seat broke, I didn't bother to fix it. I simply drove the car until it could drive no more. I didn't think it was worth much else than that.

Haven't we all had those moments when we decided to drive it until the wheels fall off, whatever "it" is?

Ride out the depression.

Keep overeating the food that's bad for us.

Engage in the same fight with our spouse over and over.

Refuse to try at our job.

Sabotage ourselves just when things start to work out.

But this behavior always ends the same way: with us worse off than when we started.

How we start might be different. For some of us that moment comes after that sip of alcohol or that fight with our spouse or that biting loneliness that shows up at 2:00 a.m. when the house is quiet. But it always ends the same: with our believing we're too broken to be fixed. We're a 1984 Chevy Citation, in electric blue and maroon, not worth the effort to repair. Not worth working on.

But think about this: it's never God telling us we're too broken. It's someone else. The parent who failed us, the friend who let us down, the message we received after walking away from hurt. One writer in the Bible (who suffered plenty, believe me) says, "The Lord is close to the brokenhearted and saves those who are crushed in spirit" (Ps. 34:18). Think about how different that is from the way people have treated you in the past.

But sometimes it's us telling ourselves these lies. We have decided that we are an ugly used car that is broken beyond repair. So instead of putting in the time and effort to fix the seat or replace the hubcap, we've given up. We've chosen to drive ourselves into the ground. Instead of working to better ourselves or create a healthier life, we quit. We medicate with negative behaviors. We self-sabotage. This leaves us feeling like we're either constantly failing or less than those around us.

We begin to believe that we're not worth anything because

we're broken, that it's better to drive ourselves until we can't drive anymore rather than put in the effort to make ourselves better.

This reminds me of the people on *Antiques Roadshow*. In case you haven't seen that TV show, it features people bringing in old or antique items they think might have value to get them appraised by experts. They want to see whether they have a priceless artifact or just junk. Occasionally, people learn that the item they've brought in is rare or of historical value or worth a tremendous amount of money.

What I find fascinating about the show is how people present items to the appraiser when they don't think their stuff is worth much. They bring in what they found in their attic or was passed down to them in an old box or a torn bag. They talk about the item like it has seen better days. But when they learn that the thing they brought in is actually worth a lot of money, everything changes.

Suddenly, the item is an heirloom and the person holds it differently. What's funny is that the item itself hasn't changed in the least—it's still dusty and falling apart—but the individual's perception of its value has done a complete one-eighty.

Doesn't this ring so true in our own lives? How many of us treat ourselves like something discarded and found in an attic, when in reality we're priceless art. Our brokenness—our past, our mistakes, our failures—doesn't determine our value, God does. His spirit toward us is something like the prophet Isaiah's description of God's attitude toward his people: "Since you are precious and honored in my sight, and because I love you, I will give people in exchange for you, nations in exchange for your life" (Isa. 43:4).

Think about how beautiful that is. Something I've learned about myself and about the people I've worked with as a therapist is that we don't always have someone in our lives to give us permission to be okay.

Growing up, I loved, and still love to this day, self-help books on personal development and growth. I love reading about how to dress, how to be, how to succeed. But unfortunately, that created in me the idea that I always need to be different—I need to continue to change all the time to be the best version of myself that I can be.

And I think some of us have gotten that message as children too, from our parents or other influential adults. They loved us, but we needed to change a lot to be more lovable. They'd love us more if we did things differently. We needed to fix our brokenness to have value.

I want to give you permission not to do anything. Our value in God's eyes is not contingent on what we've done or how we've changed. We are valuable in God's eyes simply because we are his sons or daughters. And he is the same God who is such a good father that the Bible says "he will wipe every tear" from our eyes (Rev. 21:4).

I think God has feelings about things. I think God would like us to change in some ways, and I think God has opinions about our actions, but we are valuable regardless of the decisions we make. We're valuable to him no matter how many wrong turns we take. For many, that truth is much different from what we were raised to believe or what we've read.

It's a powerful gift to ourselves to say, *It's okay just to be who you are. You don't have to be someone else. Your brokenness isn't about your value.*

I think this is why we often both love and despise elderly people. It seems like the older you get, the more comfortable you are with being yourself. While this doesn't always translate to being the best version of yourself in your later years (the phrase "Get off my lawn!" comes to mind), age brings a certain confidence in knowing who you are. As we age, we realize that we don't have the time to pretend or contort ourselves into someone that others might like better. Instead, the focus becomes (or at least should become) living well with the personal qualities we have rather than asking for new ones.

A good friend of mine put this more directly to me over coffee one day. This friend had recently retired and said that at the end of the day, "you are who you are, and happiness starts with accepting that fact." That is so true. From that foundation we can build on our strengths and weaknesses and certainly improve, but the first thing we have to do is accept ourselves. If we don't accept ourselves, no one else will.

What's fascinating is that if you ask any person eighty years old or older about who they are or who they dreamed of being, they will typically tell you that as a child their sole goal was to survive. It can be easy to forget that there were decades here in the US, and in many other countries, when there was little time or space for personal development and aspiring to be someone else. Instead, the focus of this generation was simply on maximizing what you had and using it to survive. I think this mindset might be more helpful than the self-help we're constantly fed about realizing our value as a person.

Maybe there are things in your life that you really need to change. But there are also things you don't need to change, regardless. You are valuable no matter what.

I wish I'd heard that more often growing up. I wish my parents had told me that. I wish I would tell my kids that more. We're missing this message today. Our culture communicates the message that we do need to change, always. If we identify a problem, we need to solve it immediately or something's wrong with us.

I don't say this to encourage bad behavior. I don't want to encourage a lack of motivation or complacency either. But you have to hear me: you have value. Your worth is incredible in the eyes of God. No matter what you've done. No matter what has been done to you. No matter what messages you believe about yourself. Regardless of whether you do anything to improve yourself.

You're not a 1984 Chevy Citation with a missing hubcap, unworthy of being fixed. And when we realize this, we can understand the confidence that comes not from pretending to be someone else but from loving who we really are.

Do you have a person or people in your life you can look to for encouragement and acceptance? Are you one of those people? The easiest way for others to see value in who we are is if we believe we have value first. Just like on *Antiques Roadshow*, our perception of our value often dictates how we talk about and carry ourselves. If you struggle to see your value, ask a friend or loved one what you are missing. I'll bet they have some ideas for you to consider.

Chapter 4

SOMETIMES OUR PAST ISN'T OUR FAULT

Sometimes our brokenness isn't our fault. And that's a total bummer.

When our brokenness is our fault, we can at least take responsibility for what we did. We don't have to wrestle with how the person who injured us will handle what they did. We don't question whether they will address what happened, and in some ways that's a comfort. The ball is in our court when it's our fault.

But when we're broken because of someone else's actions, we are left to choose how to react, and that can be difficult.

What do I mean when I talk about a brokenness that isn't our fault?

Maybe you were abused as a kid.

Your spouse cheated on you.

A friend cut you out of their life for no reason.

Your dad was an alcoholic.

You were in foster care.

People talked about you behind your back.

Your parents got a divorce.

None of these things are your fault, but you still have to deal with the fallout. You still have to deal with the brokenness that resulted from someone else's poor decisions or mistakes.

This reminds me of a friend named Jack, who has some significant health problems. He played a lot of sports growing up and enjoys being active and outside, but since he learned he has multiple sclerosis, he hasn't been able to do a lot of the things he enjoys. While he is fortunate that the disease hasn't yet debilitated him, it's an ever-present concern in his life.

Jack didn't ask for this disease, but he approaches his new limitations with the realization that everyone's got "something" in life. There are somethings we can see and others we can't, but for us to dream that we don't have something is, unfortunately, just that, a dream.

Watching Jack take his medication every month, which costs thousands of dollars, and continue to smile and say, "Yeah, I can do that" or "I can do some of that" when I ask him to hang out with me has been eye opening. His attitude has helped changed my perspective on brokenness.

Imagining how I'd feel if I had this disease attacking my body in my thirties, I asked him if he was angry.

He said, "Jason, there are so many things I could be angry about and so little time. I haven't spent time doing that yet."

As a procrastinator, I can totally relate to this—putting something off—but then he reiterated that there simply isn't enough time to waste being upset about what we can't control.

I know that this point—focus only on what you can change or have control over—is probably overused by now, but it's so true. We so often get stuck on the fact that we can't control what's happening to us.

Jack can take medication, he can deal with it, he can live with it if he chooses to, or he can let it overtake his life. Those are his choices. But he can't control that it happened to him. So to hear him say, "Yes, I could spend a lot of time being angry about this, but it's ultimately out of my hands. I can't do anything about it," is refreshing. He's not giving up, he has simply accepted that he can't control everything that happens to him and has chosen to move forward.

I think it's important that we walk this line between accepting what has happened and honoring our ability to choose. We were not able to choose what happened to us in the past. But we *are* able to decide how to respond to it today.

Your parents got divorced. You have a choice when it comes to your relationships.

Your dad was an alcoholic. You can decide how to approach alcohol.

You were abused. You can choose whether to deal with that hurt in a healthy way.

For me one of the most interesting aspects of being a therapist has been working with people who have committed serious crimes. Shortly after leaving school and beginning my journey to become a licensed therapist, I worked with people who had committed a sex offense, as well as with victims of sex offenses. It was difficult work and not for the faint of heart.

When I first began working with victims of abuse, I expected to find that they would want the person who hurt them to have a terrible life. But what I found early on is that many of the victims wanted the person who hurt them to be able to change, to go on and have a better life even though their crime had had a significant unfixable impact on their own life. They often surprised me by saying something like, "I want the person who hurt me to be able to deal with their issues and become successful, because if they're successful, I feel like change has occurred and some good came of my pain."

I was shocked that a person could look at what had happened to them, something heinous, something that would make the news, and wish for a better outcome for the person who had hurt them. I was dealing with some of my own brokenness at the time, some stuff that had happened to me that I hadn't asked for and never wanted. I remember talking with someone who said to me, "Why would I want the person who wounded me so badly to go on to have a miserable life? Then nothing good comes from the situation. Why would I want to have a miserable life? If I go on to have a miserable life, there's nothing left."

I realize that sounds terribly simple. Just want the best for the person who hurt you, forgive them, and you won't have to deal with the brokenness they caused anymore. Easy, right? But that's not everyone's story. Maybe you've been hurt by someone and are in a season when what you want most is for that person to hurt too. That emotion makes sense and is valid, but ultimately this is a costly way to deal with a painful situation. The only way light can ever shine through this kind of darkness is if we take the next step to do the right thing.

So much of our brokenness is the result of other people's woundedness. That doesn't make what they did to us right; it doesn't justify it or give anyone an excuse. But there's this saying: hurt people hurt people. I tend to agree but would add that hurt people who haven't done the work hurt people. If we're not careful, things that happened to us that we didn't ask for—our parents' divorce, abuse, illness, disability—can take us from being the victim to hurting someone else. We all know the cycles of pain that people "pay forward." If we don't deal with our brokenness, even brokenness that wasn't our fault, we will end up hurting those around us because we didn't deal with our pain. That's the really unhappy ending.

We all want to be happy, yet happiness is not always part of life. We will struggle at times; we will have pain and brokenness. Sometimes we will cause other people's brokenness, and sometimes other people will cause ours. The blueprint for healing our brokenness is the same as for healing brokenness we've caused others. We must acknowledge what's true, accept it, process it, do what we can to make the situation as okay as it's going to be, and then move on.

If we don't move on from whatever was done to us, we end up making it our permanent state of life. We'll live as wounded, broken, damaged people, and nothing else.

I often tell my clients to think of their brokenness as a season at a terrible summer camp they were forced to attend. At the camp there are programs to follow, songs to sing, ways to behave to get through camp. But at the end of the season, we leave—until the next time we have to go there. The point is never to live at summer camp forever. For better or for worse, it ends and you move on. You'll look back later at the time you spent there and feel something about it, but that time has passed. The season has changed.

If you've experienced brokenness, I'm not saying you should just get over it, I'm inviting you to work through it. Because if we don't make an effort to get through it, we'll get stuck, as if in hardened amber. Encapsulated wounds can define our lives, robbing us of the joy and fulfillment we desire.

There was a season in my life when I would have read what I just wrote and thought it was a bunch of garbage. I would have angrily closed the book and said to myself, *This guy doesn't get it. It sounds too simple.* And in some ways, it is too simple, because it starts with a choice.

When we're hurt, we have to decide to make our lives bigger than the pain we were caused.

Our lives are bigger than the person who left us.

Bigger than the abuse.

Bigger than the illness.

Bigger than what people think.

But it's a choice we'll have to make over and over. We'll have to scream it, cry it, whisper it, say it boldly. And when we've said it enough times to enough people who love us, it will get easier.

My life is more than _____.

Eventually, you'll be able to make that statement with confidence because you have come to believe it. And when you can do that, your life will have changed. The wound may still be there, just like my friend's disease is still there, but the way you see the wound is different. You will realize that you have made it into something far more beautiful than it could have been on its own.

Instead of a scar, you have made your wound into a birthmark that reminds you of your decision to live for more.

> Do you need to make a different choice? What is one step you can take today toward living that new choice?

30

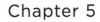

Chapter 5

BUT SOMETIMES IT IS OUR FAULT

When I was a kid I got really into rollerblading—not just rollerblading down the sidewalk, not rollerblading simply for recreation, I got really into doing tricks.

Maybe it was just because I grew up in the Midwest, but rollerblading tricks seemed really risky and exciting. And as a kid, risky and exciting were exactly what I was going for.

I had this pair of red rollerblades that I loved to death. They were ugly. I still have a picture of me holding up these red rollerblades that's just terrible. But in my mind, I looked fantastic wearing them and doing all my tricks.

I would clear the stairs. Do grinds or rail slides. Attempt jumps —not major ones but ones I could handle. I felt like the professional skaters I saw in the movies and on TV, and it was amazing.

One day I went downtown with some friends to skate, because downtown is the coolest place to skate as a sixteen-year-old, right? We skated around, jumped some stairs. I'm sure the onlookers we attracted with our sweet tricks were just so thrilled and feeling lucky they got to watch me.

Then we came up to one set of stairs, about six steps, and decided to jump them. Six steps, that was a big deal for me. My friends and I skated to the edge, looked down, walked to the bottom, looked up—pretty much did all the things you're supposed to do as a kid when you're about to do something stupid—and decided this might be a good idea. I knew I could pull this jump off. So I went back to the top and backed up a bit so I would have more than enough clearance, then skated as hard as I could toward the stairs. As I got to the edge of the steps, I jumped.

Now, we're talking a millisecond here, but in that moment, I was flying. It was amazing. I was at the height of my rollerblading career. This was as good as it was going to get. What's more, I landed the jump! (Well, I was dragging my foot a little bit at the end, but I still pulled it off. I jumped those steps.)

I was elated. So much so that I kept rolling and jumped off the curb and sailed out into the street right into a patch of wet cement. Yeah, that's right. Despite all of our scouting before the jump, we failed to notice that near the stairs, a crew had poured cement that was still drying.

So after my elation, I was quickly disappointed. I had glided into wet concrete and now my beautiful red rollerblades were covered with the stuff.

What's worse is that I took several big steps while I was in the wet cement because, obviously, I didn't want to get stuck. Those steps completely wrecked the smooth surface.

No sooner had I jumped out of the wet concrete than I saw the construction crew coming back from their lunch break. They weren't too thrilled to see me. I'm not sure what I expected, but a little applause for the jump I'd just landed wouldn't have hurt. Had they seen the trick, I think they might've been impressed.

It would've been worth it. But man, they were not impressed. Instead, they started yelling at me. And they weren't looking for autographs.

To top things off, a police officer nearby heard the commotion. He overheard me saying "I'm sorry" over and over again and saw my face turning bright red, then noticed my Ronald McDonald–red skates and the construction workers yelling at me, and decided to come over. He sympathized with me a little bit, but ultimately he just said, "Man, you ruined all that concrete."

He offered to take me and my rollerblading buddies home. By this point I was having one of the best, worst days of my life. I was very excited about the jump—the biggest jump I'd ever made—but as I rode home, I just felt this extreme sense of guilt. These guys had worked hard, probably all day, to pour that section of concrete. I had ruined all that work with a stupid jump that was really just about stroking my ego. I hadn't known the concrete was wet. I hadn't meant to hurt them and their work. But I did.

Sometimes it is our fault—our brokenness, our past, our mistakes, the brokenness of others. Ruining a section of concrete with an ill-timed jump is a small-scale example, but it's still true: sometimes there's no one to blame but ourselves. It happens and it stinks, but it's part of the deal.

It's challenging when we have only ourselves to blame. We creatively try to blame others for whatever we're experiencing, but in the middle of the night when we can't sleep, we know it was our fault. And that hurts.

But realizing when you're responsible for your own brokenness is part of living well. Growth often leads to insight about our choices, and then, often, to some regret. Though this regret is uncomfortable, it's also part of the healthy life we are trying to build. Our job is to own what we can own and leave the rest behind, commit to change, take responsibility, and have compassion and grace for ourselves.

I don't know about you, but some days I struggle to reconcile who I was with who I am today (especially when thinking about my past rollerblading self). I look back at decisions I made and recognize that my behavior hurt some people significantly. What's worse, I see there's little room for resolution or not enough connection at this point in our lives to ask for forgiveness.

So what do you do when this is the case?

You have to learn from those mistakes and move forward, honoring those you hurt. The hard part is that this kind of living doesn't often feel all warm and fuzzy like you think it should. Instead, it often feels unresolved and less-than in a world where we like to keep everything in nice little boxes.

What can you do if you look in the rearview mirror and see only miscalculations, poor judgment, and even egregious behavior? You can start by owning and taking responsibility for the parts that were your fault.

The first time I met my friend Terry was while I was managing a staffing company. You could just tell by looking at him that Terry wasn't a fella to mess around with. He had quite a few prison tattoos and a nasty scar by his eye. He was not a guy you'd expect to see at JCPenney selling khakis or at a staffing company looking for a job.

That's probably because Terry had just been released from prison after serving twenty years for murder.

The whole prison-time-for-murder thing is usually not a great lead-in if you want to get a job. But something about Terry seemed different. He took an application from my desk and sat down to fill it out. About thirty minutes passed before he came back to my desk with the application and some scribbles on the page. To be honest, part of me thought, *This is never going to happen for this guy*, but then Terry surprised me. He told me he struggled his whole life with reading and writing and asked for my help filling out his paperwork because he really wanted to work.

I sat down with Terry and my mind changed about him.

Terry told me that he had made almost every mistake that a person could make. Having committed murder at a young age, Terry had lived most of his life in prison, but that reality didn't initially change his behavior. Instead, Terry said, one day he had a conversation that changed his life.

He was talking with a businessperson who was visiting the prison. The visitor told Terry he still had a lot of life left to live and could choose a different legacy. Terry told me that for some reason it had never occurred to him that he had a choice in the direction the rest of his life took. Terry said that growing up on a tribal reservation, he had always felt that a certain kind of life had chosen him rather than that he had chosen a life for himself. So when that businessperson told Terry he could decide which life to choose, it felt like the world opened up for him. But so did the anguish and guilt because of what he had done.

Terry believed his best hope was to start living a life that reflected goodness so that at the very least if the people he hurt saw him, they would know he had changed. He didn't think this new lifestyle would ever be enough to make up for the crimes he'd committed, but it was what he could do, and so he vowed to do that at the very least.

Terry accepted that his brokenness was his fault, but he didn't let it stall him. Despite huge obstacles, Terry persevered and built a life to be proud of.

Maybe you're reading this and thinking that if people only knew how badly you had messed up your life, they wouldn't be telling you to try to change.

You're too far gone.

You're too broken.

Too many things were your fault.

You've hurt too many people.

I understand. And yet change is still possible.

Some of us are late bloomers. We take a long time to learn through trial and error what people told us not to do in the first place. This can be a painful way to live, but it happens. The key here is that the minute you realize it's your fault is the same minute you can go out and start to change.

Like Terry, the world might be a challenging place for you. But you can show up, take responsibility for your actions, and ask for help to build a better life.

Unfortunately, I lost track of Terry, but last I heard he was working full time and had his own apartment. During our last conversation, he shared how excited he was to get to pay taxes. Terry might not know it, but his decision to take responsibility for his brokenness changed a lot of lives, and your decision can too.

When we do the hard work to recognize that sometimes

our situation is a result of our choices, we can move forward to attempt to heal the wounds we've inflicted, or at least to move forward even when what we've done can't ever be fixed. And when the wounds (or the wet cement you've skated into) can't be healed, we learn to honor those we've hurt by changing for the better and living an honorable life.

Take a minute to think through a mistake that has stuck with you. Is it time to forgive yourself and let it go? Our mistakes are often viewed in concrete terms, as if they make us failures or say something about our character when really they don't. They're just mistakes. What mistake can you make it a point to let go of this week?

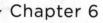

Chapter 6

DON'T RUN FROM THE BROKENNESS

When our daughter, Isla, was a baby, she was diagnosed with hip dysplasia. We were told that the joint that held her hip in the socket was shallow, and therefore her hip could become easily dislocated.

As young parents, my wife and I felt panicked. How could such a thing have happened? We were told it happens sometimes. There wasn't really anything or anyone to blame. But we still needed to take action, and it would be hard.

Our beautiful baby girl had to be put in a body cast. The cast set the hip and went up to her chest, so she could grow out of it. The hope was that setting the hip and making sure it didn't dislocate would allow her hip socket to develop more fully so that Isla would later be able to live a normal life without surgery.

It would be four months. She could already crawl, and it became difficult for us to think about all the things she could no longer do. It still pains me today. During this time, Isla also had to learn how to sleep differently. She was uncomfortable and confused. You obviously can't communicate very well to a baby why she's suddenly being forced to do something totally different from what she knows. This was such a challenge. But soon she learned to live with the cast. She pulled herself along, dragging her body cast. It required a tremendous amount of strength to pull her whole body, plus a cast, around on the floor, but she did it anyway. She learned to sleep differently. She learned how to sit up with the cast, tipped like a giggling bag of groceries, leaning up against things and using the cast as sort of a built-in chair. Over time all these different ways of doing things became normal to her. It was what she knew.

Maybe she didn't know the difference, but instead of choosing to give in to her brokenness, Isla embraced it and kept going. That was the season she was in—she had to wear this cast to make herself better. Had she not worn the cast, it was pretty certain that she would have had to undergo a series of surgeries to fix her hip problem.

Eventually the cast came off. After anxiously awaiting the news, we learned that the therapy had been successful. The socket had developed the way it was supposed to. She would not need the surgery. We were elated. And since that time, Isla has lived a normal life. We've had her hip checked up on and she's been okay. And there's more. She's developed a resilience, demonstrated so many times since then, that I'm certain is from this experience as a baby. She feels pain, she gets wounded, but at the same time, she seems to know that she will make it. After all, there are seasons when we have to wear a cast to reset, and then there are seasons when we can remove the cast and thrive.

Sometimes we're tempted to run from any kind of brokenness or hard thing we face. But what if brokenness could make us better? My daughter is better because of the brokenness she walked through as a baby. Not just healthier but a stronger person emotionally and mentally too. What if brokenness is the one thing you need to walk through to get to healing on the other side?

Other times we run away from something when we don't need to. I remember taking a trip to Florida with Jodi. It was one of the first trips we got to take together after having kids, so it was pretty amazing just getting some time to hang out and reconnect. We started the trip by going to the beach (which obviously you do on the first day when you're from South Dakota). When we got down on the sand, we really didn't think about much besides being somewhere warm and having fun. We certainly didn't think too much about sunscreen. After all, we weren't going to be out for more than thirty minutes. Well, thirty minutes was enough. It turns out sunscreen is always a good idea. We got terribly sunburnt that day at the beach, and so had a miserable, crispy couple of days, slathering aloe vera on our sunburns every other hour.

A few days into this, when we were finally feeling better, Jodi and I walked to a bakery we had found earlier. We love good food and Jodi is a wonderful chef, so we're always searching for something new to try or a place that's known for being really good. We had heard about this bakery in Florida run by people from New York that had great bagels, so we bought some bagels and walked back to our hotel. We had to go over this drawbridge that lifts up whenever big boats pass through. For whatever reason, this drawbridge provoked anxiety for me. I just thought about how you never really know when it might lift up for a boat to go underneath. At least that was my fear as we walked up to the bridge.

As we were crossing the bridge, we heard a guy yell, "Hey!" and the light on the bridge started flashing. We took off running, not back to where we came from, mind you, but all the way across the rest of the bridge. Why? I don't know. It just seemed like a better idea to get across the three-fourths of the bridge we had left than to head back.

So we were running, running, *running*, trying to get across the bridge before it opened and we fell to our tragic deaths (at least that's what I was imagining), only to see that the bridge wasn't opening. Once we were on the other side, safe and sound, we realized that the guy who yelled was just calling to a coworker a little farther down the bridge.

We had been sprinting from what we thought was "hey, the bridge is opening and you're going to fall into the ocean" when it was actually just "hey, I need you (not you, Jason) for something." We'd thought we were running away from certain injury or maybe death when instead we were running into danger. We were just these bright red midwesterners sprinting across a bridge because we were certain we were in trouble.

Our brokenness can be like that sometimes. Brokenness can make us feel in danger. It can say something's really wrong. So we run from it, when it would probably be more helpful just to look at it. If Jodi and I had taken even just a second to look back at the guy who was yelling, we would have established who he was talking to. We didn't have to run. We could have just walked.

We don't need to run from our past, our mistakes, our problems. Instead, what would happen if we looked our brokenness dead in the face? What if we confronted it straight on? So much additional brokenness, like shame, regret, hiding, and embarrassment, could be avoided—at least that's what I've found in my own life.

Not so long ago I visited my good friend Bob Goff at his newly opened retreat center, The Oaks, in California, where another friend, Mike Foster, was hosting a couples' retreat. I say these men are friends, but what's also true is that they are mentors, coaches, and heroes of mine. It would be an understatement to say that I was excited to go. On our way out there, I had some problems at the airport, which included my passing out and throwing up because of a chronically low heart rate and a little too much caffeine (I said I was excited), which led to a rescheduled flight and some waiting time. So when I was finally able to get on that plane, man, was I elated.

What's more, I was thrilled to have Jodi along with me because it was a marriage retreat. And—you're going to love this—even though I'd been a therapist for years, this was the first marriage retreat we had ever attended. Aren't therapists supposed to love retreats like that? Of course! We just hadn't gotten around to going to one yet. I was filled with hope and excitement for the retreat. What would I learn? How would Jodi and I connect? What would we do? This was going to be amazing. I had the highest of hopes.

We traveled to the retreat center, saw my good friend, met some new friends, and everything was going wonderfully—right up until we had a breakout session in which we started to talk about some difficult things. For me, when hard things come up, I have to be careful, because these types of conversations are often triggering. When that happens, if I'm not focused, my brokenness and trauma can sometimes spill over. Maybe you can relate?

And that's exactly what happened during this breakout session with Jodi. I wish I could tell you that we were having a really important conversation, that we were strategic about our conflict, that I said the right thing and hit on the correct points. I don't even really remember what we started fighting about, to be honest.

But over the course of this afternoon, when we were supposed to be laughing in the sun, swimming, and doing all these amazing things at the retreat center, I found myself fighting with my wife in our cabin, fighting like we hadn't fought in years. We covered all of our greatest hits—you know, the things you never resolve that just keep coming up. This was not what I'd expected of our first marriage retreat, and when I yelled that maybe we needed to sleep separately for a while when we got home, I knew I had gone too far. Way too far.

You can't just say something like that and then ask the other person to put sunscreen on your back. If we were at home, maybe I could have just hidden my feelings or gone somewhere for a little bit, but we were at a marriage retreat with a bunch of other couples, and the reality is that the minute I said it, I crushed Jodi's feelings. I frantically tried to think of how to solve this problem quickly, or how to at least put a bandaid on it so we could pretend it had never happened and go on with the weekend. Unfortunately, it was less of a bandaid situation and more like the time I kicked a soccer ball through our picture window while my mom was gone and I tried to hide it by hanging a towel over it. The window was still broken, and my mom and everyone else knew it.

Eventually we concluded that we were getting nowhere, that we weren't even sure what we were arguing about anymore.

I was sad that I had said hurtful things to Jodi, but the retreat was still going on and I couldn't just hole up in the cabin for the rest of the trip. I couldn't be the guy who was like, "Hey, can you just leave some food at the front door? I know we came here to see friends and attend this retreat, but could you just leave me alone?"

So instead of hiding like I so desperately wanted to, we stepped out of the room and headed to meet everyone at the pool. I was terrified—terrified that I would be seen, terrified that everyone would know how broken we really were. As we walked, we ran into Mike and his wife, whom I have long respected and admired from afar and now hoped to become friends with. I stood there and could only think, "I'm caught."

Because neither Mike nor his wife are mind readers, they asked, "How's it going?"

When people know you, or when they actually care, or when they're good listeners, or when they're a therapist too, "How's it going?" becomes a dangerous question because they actually want to know how it's really going.

I had a second to decide. Should I try to hide the brokenness that had just occurred between me and Jodi? Should I lie about it? Should I push it to the side? Should I call it something else? Or should I just own it?

This might not seem like that big of a deal to you, but in that moment I felt as exposed and vulnerable as ever. It was like meeting one of your heroes and telling them you're actually really messed up and hoping they still like you. I attribute what happened next to God, because if it had been up to me, I don't think I would have said what came out of my mouth. I leveled with Mike and said, "Today has been terrible. We fought. I said some things that were really unkind. I'm embarrassed. I don't know what to do."

This was hard for me to admit, and I'm almost certain that after I said it, I winced. I just expected that they would think less of me because of what I'd just told them. But they didn't. Instead, Mike said, "Oh? What can we do to help? Let's talk it out. What's going on?"

My friend didn't reject me when I showed him my brokenness. He welcomed me with open arms.

So often our temptation is to run away from our brokenness, whether that means ending a relationship, relocating, or simply not returning a call. And yet when we do this, nothing changes. There is no improvement. Instead it just becomes another place we don't go.

It's challenging, but sometimes we need to stay put and deal with the brokenness. Maybe because we are tired of running or we are in too much pain, but it becomes obvious that it's time to do the work.

Is there something on your heart today that you need to work on? Do you have a towel hanging over a broken window somewhere that you need to take down? I know that feeling all too well. It can seem like we are so busted and broken that we will never be okay again. But here's the thing: the only guarantee that you won't move on is if you keep trying to convince yourself and others that the towel isn't really there.

When you risk letting a therapist, coach, friend, or other safe person in, what you often find is that you are hardly alone. In most cases, the person understands and wants to help you get put back together. We let shame and guilt hold us back from letting others in, which can lead us to feel isolated and without hope. Perhaps the best way I've found to get closer to talking to someone is to tell God what's going on. Although he already knows, it's a powerful way to build some confidence to share something in a place where you will never be rejected. After you've had that conversation with God, the next step usually is much more accessible.

Take a couple of minutes to identify whether there is something you need to share with God. If there is, find a quiet place and meet him there. Tell him the truth about things and how you feel, and pray about who to talk to next. Know that you are loved no matter what and are never alone.

Chapter 7

FEEL IT TO HEAL IT

Anyone who's gone through grief knows it's a roller-coaster ride.

I was flying back from working in Nashville, which typically involves a brief layover in Chicago, and I was exhausted. The kids had been sick before I left, work had been tough, and I was honestly just thrilled to get to eat Swedish Fish and watch *The Office* on the plane ride home.

Somewhere around my third or fourth episode and just before the plane landed, I looked out the window. It looked like a serious storm was rolling in, and as I watched, lightning flashed. I figured it wasn't a good sign but went back to watching *The Office* and we landed like on any normal day.

As I deplaned and walked off the jet bridge, I was greeted by chaos. People were yelling at gate attendants, at each other, at their phones, at *everyone*. One man was even yelling at his dog. It was the anti-Disneyland, the exact opposite of "the happiest place on earth." I soon understood why. I looked up to see the departure board filling with flight cancellations because of the weather. Unsurprisingly, Sioux Falls was one of them. And so I joined the seemingly endless line of people waiting for customer service.

For two hours. Amid all the yelling.

When I finally got my chance at the customer-service counter, I was told that my flight was rescheduled for the following morning and that they were putting me up in the airport Hilton overnight. I thanked the attendant, imagining a nicely appointed hotel room overlooking the airfield. At the hotel, I was informed I had a boardroom suite, which contributed to my fantasy of a classy, grand-luxury detour. Sure, it was a change of plans, but I'd have something to eat, call Jodi and the kids, and get some much needed sleep.

I should have been thinking more along the lines of the movie *Planes, Trains and Automobiles*. (If you haven't seen it, let's just say that you won't envy the travelers.)

When I checked into the room, I saw that it was in fact a boardroom. There was a big table and about a dozen chairs to prove it. I did find a folding bed someone had mercifully placed next to the conference table, so I got ready for bed, planning to listen to some music before I fell asleep.

As I crawled into the squeaky rollaway, two things happened. The first is that my feet hung at least a foot beyond the edge of the bed. The second is that the Avett Brothers song "I and Love and You" started playing on my playlist. This is one I dreaded, the song that had played on repeat as we drove home from the hospital empty-handed after our adoption fell through. The pain was all right there.

Could there be a more perfect setup for a miserable night? I half expected a bathtub to come crashing through the ceiling.

As I lay there, toes exposed, waiting for something horrible to come from the shadows under the conference table and eat them, I considered changing the song. But as annoyed as I was, I just let it play. I felt tears welling up. I did my best to hold them back, doing that thing where you turn red and start to breathe weird, but eventually I gave up and let it out.

It hurt to think of that day driving home and singing to a stupid song that didn't even help at all. I thought of the loss and the grief, and I ugly cried in my little "boardroom suite" away from home.

When is this going to stop hurting?

In my exhaustion, I realized I was tired of dealing with it by not really dealing with it. I'd been trying to avoid the song and so much else besides, and I decided right then and there that I was going to do whatever I needed to make peace with what had happened. I had no clue what that meant, but I knew it was going to take more than time and a couple of halfhearted attempts to resolve it. And I hoped I might eventually reconcile with the pain.

Today I can listen to the Avett Brothers sing "I and Love and You" without tearing up, which I guess is maybe progress. I know I'll always think about that day, and Jodi does too, but it has become a hard thing we share, something that we honor for each other.

One of my wife's cousins had a child who, when he was only a couple of years old, went through a terrible bout with cancer. They held fundraisers to raise money in an attempt to save the child. They tried everything. But ultimately, the child died.

I went to the funeral. Like everyone, I had no idea what to say. The crushing feeling was indescribable. Your mind just can't believe it for a long time, even though your heart can't stop feeling like it's going to break.

That loss really triggered me, hitting all the things I had struggled with in our attempts to get pregnant. By that time, Jodi had actually gotten pregnant against all odds and we had two young children. But as I sat with hundreds of others in an auditorium that smelled like school lunch and gym shoes, I was at a loss. They showed a video montage, and one of the songs was by Mumford and Sons called "I Will Wait." Once again I had a transformative experience with a song. It so perfectly encapsulated what I was feeling. It encapsulated what I think a lot of people were feeling. And I cried.

For a long time afterward, I couldn't hear "I Will Wait" without thinking of the loss of that child. And what I've realized since is that when we're stuck, sometimes it's okay to put our feelings into a song.

It's healthy to create some sort of tradition or to find some sort of structure to hold on to those feelings. Sometimes we all need something to convey the feelings we have trouble speaking. There's real power in finding that. We have to feel our brokenness to heal it.

When I'm with Jodi and "I and Love and You" or "I Will Wait" comes on, we'll look at each other and remember what we went through. I know if I'm ever feeling sentimental about what happened, I can turn one of those songs on and remember that day. And I think that's important for a lot of reasons. It makes it easier to process the grief that is lingering and to give voice to what has happened while it is still happening without speaking it, sharing feelings we can't verbalize for whatever reason. As time goes on, it becomes all the more important to honor those experiences.

Having children has been an amazing blessing to our lives, but there are times I want to remember what happened and what it took to get us here. I don't want to let those memories fade, because they're part of the happiness now, and I think sometimes our saddest times become the foundation for some of the happiest.

Music is a powerful way to connect with the past. It might be different for you—a smell, a flavor, a piece of clothing, a season of the year. I've been able to collect some of those moments through songs, and I wouldn't connect with those experiences and memories as readily otherwise. The goal, whatever *your* connector is, is to try to be present to the changing experience of grief, to discern what you're feeling, and to let yourself find ways to do that. Sometimes the only way is through creative work, whether it's others or your own. Maybe it's a piece of art. Maybe it's a song or a film, but it's important to find a creative "box" to keep those feelings in. Because then we can visit that box any time we want to sit with those feelings and think about them. I could listen to the song on repeat and experience the healing of it, and then turn it off when I wanted to. This helped me process the grief, which became much more manageable.

There was a time when I wouldn't have wanted to hear either one of those songs. But over time I've come back to appreciating the beauty and the memories in them, mostly because Jodi was with me in those moments. We loved each other, we wanted the same things, and we were hurt together.

Sharing that with her was so comforting. There's beauty in that. When you're feeling down or going through grief, it changes who you are if you can remain present with your grief, especially if you can experience it with someone you love. It will leave you better, not worse. We all want to be able to hold on to meaningful experiences like that.

Feeling our brokenness this way can also allow us to let someone else express our feelings better than we ever could. Author Flannery O'Connor, talking about her father's death, said, "Our plans were so beautifully laid out, ready to be carried to action, but with magnificent certainty God laid them aside and said, 'You have forgotten—mine?'"* Both the loss of our adopted baby and the loss of Jodi's cousin's child were experiences that taught us this truth. God's plan to bring good out of life's pain has been magnificent. I could have written many books and never said it more accurately than O'Connor did.

We must feel our grief fully to heal it. We must look pain, loss, sorrow, brokenness right in the face and choose to feel them if there's any chance of our healing from them and moving on stronger. And we need to find help—from others and from God.

If we can let it out, feel our brokenness, and then take an active role in doing what's necessary to heal it, amazing things can happen.

---

* Flannery O'Connor, *The Complete Stories* (Franklin Center, PA: Franklin Library, 1980).

Maybe this chapter finds you in a place where you need to feel something. If you are in a safe and comfortable place, give yourself permission to feel something about a wound that you are dealing with. If it's challenging to go to that place, maybe consider a song, piece of art, or photograph that allows you to feel those feelings.

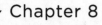

Chapter 8

FORGIVE YOURSELF AND OTHERS

I've found that one of the greatest catalysts for improvement in my life is taking responsibility for my mistakes (and there are many). Sometimes this means admitting I have no idea what I'm doing and I need help. Sometimes it means acknowledging that I know the right thing to do and just didn't do it. Other times, it means recognizing that I've been careless. Regardless, this willingness to own the truth is often the most powerful step to healing. You will not get any better than your willingness to be honest about the extent of your problems and to ask for help.

You have to get real with yourself.

It's like going to a doctor and refusing to share your symptoms, refusing to participate in further assessment, but declaring there's a problem anyway. To allow for true healing we must be willing to be honest with ourselves and show others the extent of the problem. If we do this with the right people, they might be concerned for us and possibly be hurt by our mistakes, but they will work with us toward a solution. This is the type of relationship I want for you. Whether it's a friendship, dating relationship, or marriage, it should be our goal to be both the person who is transparent and the person who receives that level of transparency without judgment and with a healthy dose of forgiveness.

But you have to realize that when you show someone close to you the wound or the extent of the problem, they might not have the best reaction. Their negative response can trigger childhood or other trauma, making you feel like they are rejecting you. But someone can reject you only as much as you reject yourself. Your behavior is just that: your behavior. It's not the sum of who you are (unless you want it to be). We all make decisions and engage in behavior that we wish we hadn't, and sometimes that behavior is appalling. Admitting this is painful, but necessary to heal, grow, and move forward.

My clients are often shocked when they work with me because no matter what they tell me they've done, my answer is always the same: "Okay. What now?" While I'd like to take credit for this approach, this is one I took from God's playbook, because when we mess up, God's answer is always the same: *I'm with you and I get it. You need to know you'll be okay.* And then, when you're ready, *Okay. So what now?* This doesn't minimize the harm done or brush it under the rug. But after proper processes of understanding and repentance, there is a path toward redemption. Sitting permanently in guilt and shame because of our behavior does nothing for anyone and, in a quiet way, denies the power of the gospel. While shame can be valid after hurting someone or ourselves, it is not the catalyst for change. The catalyst for change is awareness of the problem and the willingness to do something about it.

To get real with ourselves, we need to be willing to pursue

forgiveness for ourselves and for others, *and* be willing to change our behavior.

I learned this truth while working with felons, some of whom committed heinous and unspeakable crimes. Some of the behavior was hard even to hear about. But as I shared earlier, what I found after working with these individuals' victims was that rather than wanting the person dead, the victims often wanted the individuals who had hurt them to grow and make better choices that lead to a healthier life. When asked if the person who committed the offense should feel forever ashamed or guilty, the victims who had gone through some counseling usually wanted the person to forget about them, address the problem, and make sure they never hurt anyone again.

It's important to hear this. For those of us who have hurt someone else deeply, chances are we haven't thought that the people we've hurt might want something better for us. Instead, we believe that if we keep the candles of our shame and guilt lit for the rest of our lives, we will somehow honor those we hurt. While this might seem like a great idea, it ensures that we never let go of that harmful behavior and change. We become defined by our past. If we never forgive ourselves, we'll never be able to move on to a better, healthier version of ourselves.

Perhaps the worst part of my job is working with someone who has significantly hurt someone close to them and then decides to hold on to the guilt and shame forever. Rather than healing and growing, the person becomes more disconnected than ever and often returns to the behavior they were trying to avoid. Eventually resignation sets in, and the person just accepts that "they are who they are." In my opinion, this is the greatest loss and hurt to those they've wounded by their behavior.

Please don't do this. Instead, understand that as part of recovery, even though you will have to remember who you have been, it doesn't stop there. You don't need to carry that shame and guilt with you. Instead, you get to imagine who you are going to be.

This leads me to my next question: "Have you forgiven yourself yet?" A lot of people hear this question and give me a look that says they think I may have lost it. *How can I forgive myself for x, y, and z?* I get it. What you have done may have been immensely hurtful to yourself and others. It even may have been life altering. But still, have you forgiven yourself? If you haven't forgiven yourself, you are going to have a hard time getting others to forgive you.

Something that's awesome about God is that we only have to ask for forgiveness to be forgiven—for anything. God doesn't say he forgives only on business days or only for this or that sin. He forgives them all. Though not everyone can forgive like God can, you're not starting with everyone else. Start by seeking God's forgiveness and then work toward forgiving yourself and being forgiven by everyone else. While this might seem like a complicated process or something that requires you to take a course to learn, the reality is that it's pretty simple. In prayer, own what you've done and ask for forgiveness. Then be still and allow yourself to be forgiven. Take whatever you can from the experience and know that you are loved regardless. For people who have experienced conditional love, trauma, or abuse, this can seem like a trick, but I assure you that it isn't.

I am often asked what it means to forgive yourself. From my perspective it means making an honest assessment of what you did, taking responsibility for it and accepting the consequences, identifying what you need to change, and then changing it.

The act of forgiveness will occur many times over, sometimes in the same day, but forgiveness will happen only when paired with action. I say this because the best type of forgiveness for ourselves and others is when we can see a difference between then and now. It is difficult to forgive ourselves if we have not taken action to be different.

Let's consider an example. Say you struggle with the use of pornography. What would it look like to forgive yourself and move toward real change? First, acknowledge the extent of your struggle. Be specific about what the struggle really is, the behaviors and patterns it includes. Second, identify the consequences of your behavior. This is an important part of forgiving yourself. You must acknowledge that *you* have been hurt by your behavior. I realize that this often flies in the face of what others might tell you about forgiveness. To others, it might look like you fulfilled your own needs in a selfish and harmful way, but the behavior hurt you too. You may have hurt yourself financially, relationally, spiritually, occupationally, and so on.

You have to own it. "I was hurt by my use of pornography. Had I not been viewing it, I might have made a greater effort to engage in my marriage." Or had you not looked at porn, you might not have lost your job. Whatever ways you hurt yourself you should list. (Pro tip: there's usually a minimum of five ways that your behavior hurt you.)

After you acknowledge that your behavior has hurt you, you can move on to forgiving yourself by working to remedy the problem. Self-forgiveness does not happen while sitting in your La-Z-Boy watching TV. It happens when paired with a plan to fix the problem, such as attending therapy, participating in a group, or reading a book. Whatever you do, the point is that action is happening. The status quo isn't good enough anymore. You are pushing your comfort zone, maybe a little, maybe a lot, and getting real.

FIVE COMMON WAYS
Our Behavior Hurts Us

1. You violated your values or principles: you did something you know is wrong.
2. You traumatized yourself in the process.
3. You negatively affected or ruined a relationship that matters to you.
4. You wasted time.
5. You lost an opportunity that isn't coming back.

Only then are you able to bask in the glory of forgiveness. You are becoming a different person and have the evidence to prove it. Many people work tirelessly to receive the forgiveness of others while ignoring their need to forgive themselves.

But if we don't forgive ourselves, if we just settle into resignation, the world becomes small. There is little left to do or be curious about. Instead, we spend our time dreaming and living in a fantasy world rather than owning who we are and making changes.

Maybe today is the right time to take the first step for yourself. Make it a small one, but take it. You are worth improvement and have value.

You may be wondering why I have instructed you to seek self-forgiveness first, and the answer is twofold:

1. You have control over self-forgiveness. You only have to repent and ask.
2. When we forgive ourselves, we are able to seek forgiveness from others without making it about us.

This advice might seem to go against the grain, but time after time I have witnessed people make hollow and needy attempts at asking for forgiveness because they are asking for something they won't give themselves. Authenticity and vulnerability always come from within, and so if we don't believe we are being authentic and vulnerable, others probably won't either.

Because entire books, talks, and courses are devoted to asking for forgiveness from others, I'd like to point out that the following list of steps to asking for forgiveness hardly covers it all, but here's the gist of it:

1. Seek forgiveness from God first.
2. Identify whether the person you've hurt or harmed is interested in your apology.
   a. If they are, proceed.
   b. If they aren't, change the behavior you know was wrong and honor their decision. Remain willing to apologize should they ever change their mind.
3. Take responsibility for your behavior as specifically as possible.
4. Ask the person whether you are on the right track and whether they are willing to talk to you about their experience of what happened and let you know if you missed anything.
5. Validate their feelings and empathize as you are able.

Remember, this is about them, not you. Do not explain yourself unless they are seeking an explanation.

6. Take responsibility again if something new surfaces that you want to seek forgiveness for.

7. Tell the person specifically how you would handle a similar situation differently in the future.

8. Sincerely ask for forgiveness and accept whatever decision they make.

9. Whether they forgive you or not, change your behavior. Make your changed behavior an ongoing and living apology for and recognition of what happened.

10. Remind yourself that God has forgiven you and that your mistakes do not determine your value.

The last word on forgiveness is to be quick to ask for it. Don't let pride or stubbornness cause you to stumble further.

Is there something that you have done that you need to make peace with? A poor decision, a habit, or something worse? You know, that thing that makes you stare at the floor when a conversation gets close to touching it. That thing. Take a moment to acknowledge whatever it is and the impact it has had on you. How has it hurt you and what step do you need to take to move forward?

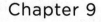

Chapter 9

TAKE BACK CONTROL

At some point we need to stop running and start healing whatever is making us feel broken. If we don't, we simply carry it with us wherever we go and it ruins new things that might have been even better.

This reminds me of the pheasant egg I kept as a kid. Growing up in South Dakota there always seemed to be a pheasant nearby, and as proof of that, I found a pheasant egg one day. Elated by my discovery, I imagined that someday the egg would hatch and I'd have my very own pet pheasant. Sure, we'd probably be misunderstood, but we'd be an *incredible* duo.

But the egg never hatched. I was as sad about this as an eleven-year-old could be, but then I forgot about it. Whenever I rearranged my room, I'd look at the egg with disappointment but then just move it somewhere new instead of getting rid of it. Eventually it came to rest in the top drawer of my dresser with my best clothes. (You know, because that's where anyone with common sense would put a pheasant egg, right?)

About a year and a half passed.

Then one day, I was in my room listening to music and having a fantastic time on an average Tuesday when I heard the faintest pop. *I wonder what that wa—* I didn't even get to finish my thought. Because the smell hit me. I think I would rate it as the worst thing I've ever smelled even today. It was as if there were a competition for the two worst smells in the world and the winning smells had a child together—that's what it smelled like. The little egg that I had refused to deal with properly had finally hatched into the smelliest goo conceivable. All over my good clothes. I was sickened not only by the smell but also by my refusal to deal with this past problem that was now causing some major present-day problems.

Want to test your marriage? Remodel your house. Seriously, it's tough work, made even more difficult by relationship problems that tend to arise right when you start swinging a hammer.

Something I learned early on about remodeling a home is you have to fix even the stuff other people can't see. This fact became evident when I was faced with a gross basement wall in a house we were remodeling. The wall looked quite dirty. Normally a perfectionist, this time I reckoned that the best thing to do would be to slap some paint on it and call it good. So that's what I did. The dirty wall was now "clean."

This method worked. For a while. The basement was dark, so I just assumed the paint had covered the rough spot and everything was fine. Until the day I walked by the wall and saw that the spot I'd painted over had come through the paint and was as ugly as ever. *What?! I painted over that spot!* The problem was that the dirty spot was not just dirty. It was moldy and mildewy. Without my having cleaned the spot first, the paint couldn't solve the problem. It just covered it up for a while.

A lot of us go through life like this. We see a dirty spot and figure that if we just throw some paint on it or avoid that area of the house, things will be fine. When this doesn't work, we now have two problems: the original problem and this new problem created by our avoidance. What I learned from the moldy-wall experience is that you have to solve the problem the first time. Throwing some paint on our issues doesn't help in the long run. And that's good, because the problem is important and worthy of our attention.

When I examine my life, I realize how much time I've spent afraid and running away from my issues. I think that sometimes when I check out, I'm probably not checking out so much as running away from a scary situation or an unwanted feeling. While I'm running from fear, I typically find myself lost and alone the way I had felt as a child. It might be oversimplifying things, but I think that at the heart of this fear is a faith issue.

I want to show that inner child that he is protected and that I am an adult now.

I want to change my relationship with fear. I don't want to keep running away from or slapping a coat of paint over my problems and calling it good.

But maybe it isn't bad to be afraid.

When I think about it, checking out and running away feels a lot like the night someone tried to break into our house.

When I was a young kid before my parents' divorce, we lived in a ranch-style house in a decent area of town. In those first years of my life, I felt safe and protected. Until that one night.

I woke up to yelling and screaming and the sounds of my

father running down to the basement. My mother was yelling that someone was trying to break in through a window. Having no concept of what was happening, I felt confused and terrified.

My father eventually came up from the basement brandishing a baseball bat and ran outside to chase the would-be intruder through the neighborhood until he got away. After that night, my life changed in many ways, but I never slept the same again. I'd wake up terrified, having to check the doors and windows even when I lived on the sixteenth floor of an apartment building.

What's funny is that I never even saw the person who was trying to break into our house. Nothing happened to me. My father saved the day by chasing him away. Nonetheless, fear followed me. I remained terrified.

I now know that this response is called trauma, but before I learned that concept, I just thought I had lost my mind. It was like being afraid of a ghost that I had never seen. It bothered me for years. So many of us have experiences that are similar to or worse than this. Something happens that changes us, but instead of seeking healing, we seek comfort, which often isolates us. Every time I checked a window or door at night, it made me feel better only in that moment. It didn't address my underlying fear or offer any type of healing.

After trauma, healthiness requires healing. Otherwise we go through our lives spending tremendous amounts of thought and energy trying to protect ourselves, even when it's unnecessary. Maybe you check a lot of doors and windows in your life because of a legitimate wound, but is that helping you? Or do you need to go back and heal instead? Most of the time healing is what needs to happen. The good news is that our heavenly Father can handle the protection part if we let him.

Imagine that every day of your life you started with a negative balance in your checking account. Wouldn't your finances feel out of control? You'd spend the whole day finding a way to get the balance to zero or just above it. Speaking from experience, I can tell you that starting the day with a negative balance is no fun. You spend your time working to make it right, whether that means getting a paycheck advance, securing a loan from a friend, or selling something at a pawn shop. It's exhausting, and even if you do everything you can, you still end the day only at zero.

A couple of years ago a bank in Florida had a computer glitch that meant their customers woke up with huge negative balances, in some cases $50,000 or more. Can you imagine? To wake up and find out that your account is $50,000 in the red? What would you do? Would you go to the gym, make breakfast, have coffee? No way! You would focus on getting the balance back to a positive amount. This is exactly what happened in Florida. Affected businesses closed for the day so they could figure things out. They couldn't stay open with such a big deficit hanging over their heads. And neither can we. When we feel this way about ourselves, it affects everything we do. To live with that hanging over your head is daunting and overwhelming.

Feeling like you always have a negative balance in your emotional bank account is often a symptom of an attachment wound—feeling abandoned in a time of need. This wound can affect us greatly in future relationships. Those of us who have this type of wound often feel like we can never measure up. No matter how much we have or how much we do, we always feel like we're battling to get to that zero balance. Sounds terrible, right? I bring attachment wounds up because they are another obstacle to healing your brokenness. To work toward healing, you must have an understanding of your struggles and the areas where you have been hurt. Without such an understanding, you may be constantly tempted to feel that you are never enough, regardless of the evidence to the contrary.

This might be a good time to talk about my friend Tony. Tony was my counselor from the time I was fourteen years old until my late teens. He helped me through some tough stuff. He was great. He was filled with God's love and was invested in helping me to heal and grow. The problem was I had an attachment wound, so eventually I moved on from Tony, even leaving unpaid a pretty big bill for his services.

A decade later, I was going to school to become a counselor. While I was searching for a local therapist to supervise me, Tony once again came into my life. To my astonishment, he agreed to supervise me, and I went into practice with him. Tony and I became close friends, and today he's one of a handful of people in my inner circle.

Because he's one of my closest friends, Tony knows I constantly struggle with feeling like my checking account is in the negative, that despite everything I have accomplished, I continue to feel that I'm not okay. He has picked up on my sometimes-annoying habit of asking him and others whether I'm okay. One night after playing a pickup soccer game together, I helped Tony carry soccer gear to his car. After closing the trunk, I sheepishly walked to the driver's-side door, where Tony was getting in. Before I could say anything to him, Tony looked at me, smiled, and said, "You're okay, Jason," shut the door, and drove off. Although I was shocked, I understood. Tony really knew me. He knew what I needed to hear and how I would attempt to get that need met.

The goal all of us with attachment wounds are working toward is to be someone like Tony to ourselves. To really do healing well, we need to identify our needs, strengths, weaknesses, and wounds and understand what we typically do to meet our needs. As you can tell by my story, we often need people close to us to help with this. But we also need to give ourselves grace and realize that everyone has needs, strengths, weaknesses, and wounds, and that it is only by looking at these things honestly that we can heal.

Looking at our wounds and the wounds of others, however, does not mean that we confront these wounds without consequences or boundaries. We need healthy boundaries and consequences in our lives, and we will talk more about those later. But the point here is that we need to fill our lives with people who really see us and love us anyway. Finding this type of person can be a challenge at times, but it's also our goal. If you don't know how to find this type of person or to create this type of a relationship, don't feel bad. You were probably just never shown how to do it. So ask.

With people in our lives who see us both accurately and objectively, we can be honest with ourselves about what is working and what we need to change. We can solicit feedback from trusted friends about who we are and how to address the things we may still be running from. And if we let people in to share the load, we can celebrate when we break out of our brokenness and take control of our healing.

Do you have people in your life who are safe to talk to about what you are struggling with? If not, how might you find them? A good way to identify people who might help is to think of someone you admire who has faced a similar problem and had success. Is there someone you need to reach out to?

PART 2

OVERCOMING
YOUR CIRCUMSTANCES

To overcome our circumstances is to change our relationship with love, because we cannot make long-term changes without having some amount of love either for ourselves or others, or both. Love is the catalyst, fuel, and glue that creates and sustains lasting change and is the difference between feeling better and being better.

But love can be difficult to grasp especially if you have been hurt by people who were supposed to have loved you. It can lead us to wonder whether love is real and, if so, what it looks like to actually find it. And strangely, although love is such an integral part of a better life, it's not often explained what it's about or how to love well.

Part 2 will guide you through the key components of healthy love and what it takes to change your relationship with your past so you can give love and receive the love you deserve.

Chapter 10

LOVE ISN'T COMPLICATED, CIRCUMSTANCES ARE

That time I got waylaid in Chicago, I was still grieving the loss of our adoption. I realized that maybe it would help to take an active role in my pain and learn to overcome it. As much as I'd grown from learning about my feelings, I knew I had to do something more.

I used to think that time was the only way to heal, but clearly healing was not so automatic. Plenty of people stay lost in their pain even though lots of time passes. I decided that knowing about my feelings wasn't doing enough to help me deal with the trauma, loss, and grief I had experienced, and so I figured there had to be a better way.

What I learned is that one of the most helpful things we can do to heal is both to experience love and to love others, because it's in that space that we really show up as our true selves and get clear about what we need to move forward. When we do this authentically, we can create relationships that are like refuges for our hearts, giving us room to walk toward healing and growth. When we are powered by love, the world looks bigger and brighter, and healing seems possible. The trouble is that often our hurt leads us away from others and toward isolation.

Here's the thing: love isn't complicated, but sometimes we are. And so sometimes we complicate the simple act of loving someone.

Our tendency to overcomplicate love makes me think of the bicycle. Since its invention in 1885, the bicycle hasn't changed much. Essentially, you sit on the seat and pedal. That's about it. Of course, the technology has changed quite a bit since 1885, and we are no longer riding bicycles that weigh a gazillion pounds and creak with every pedal stroke, but the concept is about the same.

Our goal is for love to be like the bicycle: a humble beginning that's improved on frequently but at its core is still the same.

When there is complication in love, it's usually the work that we still need to do on ourselves that's getting in the way. The more complicated love gets, the clearer it becomes that we need to take action.

I like doing intensive workshops as part of my therapy practice. In a workshop I get to spend a couple of days with someone rather than just an hour. Workshops are about more than just key takeaways and PowerPoint presentations; they're about doing. Change happens when we do something. In the doing we find that change comes easily because it has to.

For instance, how many of us, really, are confused about what it takes to eat healthy? We know. For sure, there are some nuances involved, but if we were to sit down to write out a plan for losing some weight, most of us could. We know that to lose weight, we need to eat fruits, vegetables, protein, and less sugar, and get some exercise. The problem is our unwillingness to take action.

In my practice, many times a client will discuss a behavior with a great deal of insight about what they need to do to change it. Some might say that they simply need to delete an app on their phone. And so I invite the client to delete the app right then and there. I could probably count on one hand how many times a client has actually done so.

If you're like me, you may have fantasized about someone swooping in to solve all your problems or create a perfect life that you only have to walk into. For some reason, although it seems ridiculous to me as I type this, this kind of reality always seems like a viable option to me, as if, like winning the lottery, all of a sudden everything would get easier and I'd feel great. But life and love don't work that way.

When love gets complicated, it's tempting to hope for an instant fix, but that isn't practical. What is practical is to identify what you need to do and then to move toward that goal. The goal doesn't have to be flashy or perfectly packaged. It just needs to be something we can act on.

I think often of a friend of mine who has had a lot of success in life. He has worked very hard and been otherwise frugal but has always dreamed of owning a Ferrari. So one day I got a call from my friend. "Jason, can I pick you up for a drive?" This was a bit odd since no one has picked me up for a drive since the Sadie Hawkins dance in tenth grade, but I agreed anyway.

When my friend came over, he pulled up in a 1990s Ferrari. It looked like something out of the old television show *Magnum PI*. The car was clearly a bit older, but in pristine condition, and it was, of course, a Ferrari.

How awesome! I thought as my friend pulled up. I was both jealous of him and excited to go for a ride. But then I walked up to the car and noticed that it was about four inches off the ground. *No problem*, I thought. But as I got into the car, I suddenly felt like a giant.

I had to tuck my knees up to my chest. There was nowhere to put my arms. I felt like I was trapped in a seat on a budget airline with no hope of getting a share of the armrest. It was uncomfortable.

As we pulled out of my driveway, my friend started to go through all of the quirks of the car, which sounded a lot like complications.

"You have to watch dips in the road, so it doesn't bottom out. You can't drive it in the rain." And on and on. There were an awful lot of quirks about this car that didn't actually sound that great.

As we were driving, I started thinking about love. (I realize probably only a therapist would ride in a Ferrari and think about love, but just go with it.) Sometimes we envision love to be this perfect thing, but when we get up close, it's complicated and a lot different from what we need.

It doesn't really suit us.

It's overly complicated and requires us to behave differently than we normally would.

It's cramped and doesn't allow us to grow.

(I should probably note that I love the look of Ferraris, and I'm in no way putting Ferraris or Ferrari owners down; it's just a good illustration.)

My friend ended up selling the Ferrari not long after he drove me around that sunny afternoon. I asked him why and he said that the car was just way too complicated for what he needed, and he realized those quirks weren't worth it for him.

Here's the thing: when you're in a healthy relationship, it will fit what you need and give you room to grow. You won't have to bend or contort into something you are not for it to work. It will just work.

Some of us never saw this kind of love in our childhoods. Instead, we saw my friend's Ferrari kind of love with all of its "quirks," or maybe not even that. Maybe we didn't have love in our lives at all and we were just stranded by the side of the road trying to figure it all out. I'm sorry if that was the case. You deserved more, and I'm sorry you didn't get it.

Just know that there's a healthy love that can meet your needs. It doesn't come around every day, and it's something you have to know a bit about to find.

If this all sounds like something you haven't experienced but would like to, now might be a good time to ask who can help you identify this kind of love and work toward that kind of relationship.

Take a minute to write down who you know who does love really well. A better question might be, Who loves in a healthy way that you'd like to model? Start there. Talk to that person about your experiences and learn from them.

Chapter 11

VULNERABILITY MAKES LOVE GROW

It's impossible to talk about love without talking about vulnerability. Vulnerability is emotional exposure that includes uncertainty. An example of vulnerability might be going beyond small talk with a friend to talk about something deep or meaningful to you.

Love thrives on vulnerability, and yet many of us struggle with being vulnerable. This is because vulnerability requires finesse. Sometimes we are too vulnerable with the wrong people and get hurt. Other times we're not vulnerable enough and get rejected. What's more, being vulnerable doesn't always feel awesome. Instead, it often feels a lot like risk and discomfort, and that's a tough sell.

I've learned that most couples' problems are problems with vulnerability. The less vulnerable we are, the more likely we are to become isolated and use unhealthy coping behaviors (whether or not they are romantic behaviors). The more our behavior gets out of hand, the more disconnected we become from others, including from God.

Why is that? The more we try to meet a need in an isolated way, the more we feel disconnected from others. This can lead us to feel a profound sense of loneliness. This loneliness is often the result of ongoing efforts to cope with an unmet need, which leads to guilt and shame, making it difficult to connect with others.

Our tendency to avoid vulnerability and isolate is so common that when I speak to churches and organizations, I tend to spend most of my time talking about how to connect rather than unhealthy coping. The minute I start to talk about what people do instead of being vulnerable and asking for what they need, my listeners begin staring at the floor or start to get restless in their seats. Why do we react like that?

While it might feel good to be known, it doesn't feel good when what's known is something we are ashamed of. Adam and Eve probably felt this way when they were hiding from God in the bushes. The funny thing is, God had already seen them and sought them out anyway. Most of our relationships are like that too. We just don't realize it.

It's a given that God is on our team regardless. No matter what you do, God wants to know you. (To give just one example, look up 1 John 3:1!) This is amazing and wonderful, but it's also hard to believe, especially if our parents didn't show us a similar love in our childhood. If as a child you felt you had to, or perceived that you had to, behave a certain way to obtain your parents' love, it can be difficult to believe that airing your dirty laundry would make others stick around and love you for who you are.

Let me make it clear: if you did not grow up feeling like your parents loved you regardless of your behavior, I am sorry. You should have been loved unconditionally. I am not here to blame them or to justify their behavior, but I want you to understand that if this fear of vulnerability applies to you, that shouldn't have been the case. You should know what it's like to feel like a screwup but still look into your parents' eyes to see love from them, not contempt. If you did not get to experience this love, you may have grown up believing that you are only as good as your last good deed. While this may have played a role in developing a good work ethic or attention to detail, it also taught you to withhold the things about yourself you think people may not like.

I get it. I really do. When I began working at Bethesda Workshops in Nashville to help others struggling with their sexual behavior, part of the interview process required me to share my story. This fact alone made me second-guess the whole thing. How could people want to work with me if they knew where I had come from? It seemed counterintuitive to me. Couldn't they just let me project the best version of myself like you do in any other interview and leave it at that? That wasn't the way things were going to work here, though, and ultimately I'm glad.

I decided in the weeks leading up to the Bethesda interview that I was all in, even if I walked away feeling like an idiot. So, notes in hand, I nervously recalled my story of drinking too much, acting out, being abused, and struggling to grow up to those interviewing me. The funny thing is, they didn't throw me out or even appear to judge me. Instead, they gave me a hug, prayed for me, and offered me a job. Since that interview, those same people have become some of my dearest friends. This is how it is supposed to be when you tell people the things you don't want anyone else to know. This is what it's like to be vulnerable with safe people.

→ FIVE ATTRIBUTES ←
of Safe People

1. They are good listeners.
2. They don't try to fix you.
3. They give you space to grow.
4. They validate you but also are willing to challenge you.
5. They are willing to help, and they have experience to draw from.

My initial relationship with Jodi was not all that different from the interview at Bethesda. When we met I was fresh out of a long-term relationship during which I had been immature and kind of a jerk. I had hit rock bottom. I was a twenty-five-year-old man-child who lived with his father, drank daily, smoked pot, used porn, and went to strip clubs. Not exactly the type of guy you introduce to your grandmother.

While I didn't have much going for me on paper, I knew that I could be better and that I was called to far greater things. I just didn't know how to get there. And so for the first time in my life I leveled with someone and told Jodi both the good and the bad about me. The weird thing is, like my colleagues at Bethesda, she didn't go anywhere. In fact, my honesty seemed only to solidify the deal in Jodi's mind. She will tell you now that for her, seeing me for who I truly was allowed us to develop a level of intimacy that I hadn't ever experienced before.

Although I had no idea what I was doing at the time, I can see now, and have learned from others, that vulnerability is the fertilizer for love. The trick is deciding which plants you want to grow.

When we bought our first house, I was so out-of-my-mind excited to have my own yard that I put fertilizer on everything, including the weeds, which eventually overtook the yard and blocked the grass from growing. I learned the hard way that not everything should be fertilized. In practical (non-lawn care) terms, we first want to identify whether a relationship is healthy and safe before being too vulnerable with that person. The goal is to give the other person increasing levels of vulnerability, starting with something small to see how it's received and handled. If the person is safe, you can try again with something bigger, and so on. Just realize that the number of people who will be safe and good stewards of your vulnerability is small. And that's okay.

> Take a minute to think about vulnerability. Does being vulnerable with others come easily for you, or is it a struggle? Identify people it would be safe to be more vulnerable with. What qualifies them to be on this list? Now choose one person to have a conversation with and think of one way you might let them in a bit more than you normally do, perhaps by discussing a struggle or a dream or something else that's important to you.

Chapter 12

LEARNING TO LOVE

Think about who has loved you the best so far in your life. Who has cared for you in a healthy way and made you feel loved? And what was it that made you feel that way? Was it a particular thing they did, or was it more of an attitude or approach?

Now for a hard question: Was that person who loved you best a parent?

What I'm about to say next isn't an attempt to slam or insult your parents. But what's true is that an increasing number of people would answer the question with no. Maybe it's because of societal or cultural or any number of other factors, but now more than ever children are being raised by parents who, for whatever reason (good or bad), are not good at teaching how to love.

Maybe you can relate to this: as a kid, you may have learned some things about love that weren't healthy or helpful. Maybe you learned:

You have to be perfect.
You have to give something in return.
Love is unstable and can't be counted on.

You are not lovable just the way you are.

You have to endure abuse.

If you can relate to any of these statements, I am so sorry. You should know that you deserved better. Your upbringing should have shown you a love that you want to replicate as an adult, not a kind of love that you want to be as far away from as possible.

I have a good friend who says we are all just reacting to or reflecting our childhoods. Though this might sound like a simplistic way to look at things, I agree. Some of us enter adulthood well equipped for the world, and we desire to replicate the environment we grew up in, while others wish to create an environment that looks nothing like where we came from.

If you're wanting or needing to create something new, you are welcome here. You don't have to have it all figured out. And even if you do think you have a good idea of how to love, let's talk about some of the qualities of loving someone well.

Loving others well starts with us. It is challenging, if not impossible, to love someone well if we cannot first love ourselves. I have seen many people try to give a love to others that they do not have for themselves. Ultimately this kind of love comes across as empty and lacking. It's like listening to a sportscaster who doesn't understand the sport they are talking about. They can discuss elements of the game, but if they haven't played themselves and don't have a passion for it, their commentary doesn't connect.

For many years this was my story. My upbringing taught me many unhealthy things about love. As much as I'd like to deny it, I have replicated harmful patterns at times in my adult life.

Grace tells me that hurting others wasn't my intention and that I was simply doing what I was taught, but at some point I have to be held responsible for what I have chosen to do with what I learned, whether I wanted to learn it or not. So in my twenties I started to do the work. I met consistently with a therapist to better understand what healthy love is and how to better love myself.

One of the first things I learned about love from my therapist is that healthy love looks a lot like showing up consistently for someone without having an agenda. This kind of love was modeled for me by my friend Ryan.

Ryan and I knew each other during college and then lost touch after he graduated. We both went on with our lives, got married, and focused on building our careers and having kids. Along the way through my wife's work, I came across Ryan's contact information and was inspired to give him a call.

We eventually met for coffee and got caught up. We had a lot in common, and it was clear that we both had big dreams. The thing that struck me about Ryan was that he never wavered on being my friend. He was determined to keep showing up for coffee even if my insecure self attempted to reschedule or cancel on him most of the time in the beginning.

Over time we became close, and I learned that one of the fundamental ways you can show love to someone is by showing up consistently without any kind of agenda other than to have a relationship.

Today, Ryan and I don't talk or have coffee as often as we

used to. We now have busy families and careers. But not so long ago I had a big speaking event in town. When I got near the stage to get ready for my talk, I saw Ryan and his wife in the audience. Ryan wasn't there because I told him to be or because he wanted something, he was there because one of the tenets of loving someone well is to show up. If you want to love someone well, start by showing up for them.

The second quality of healthy love is loving without strings attached. So often the love we get and give has strings. Maybe the tradeoff is that we give something in return, or we look the other way when something happens, but either way, love with strings is not really love. It's an arrangement.

Some people love you so well it seems off-putting at first. You aren't sure whether you should trust it, so you try to push them away, just in case it's not real. My friend Adam was one of those people in my life. A successful pastor, a well-known author, and an all-around fantastic guy, he seemed to just show up in my life one day. To be honest, I don't even remember how we first connected, but over the years we have gotten closer.

Early on I told Adam that I wanted to write a book. I said it was something I had been encouraged to do and had dreamed of for a long time. Adam listened and then called his agent and a couple of other agents to see if they could help. I was flabbergasted and pretty sure there was going to be a catch, like a bill for twenty thousand dollars that he forgot to mention, or a favor expected in return. But there never was.

I talked to the agents even though I wasn't established

enough yet, and Adam said they weren't ready for me but to keep working toward getting a deal with a publisher.

A year passed and I was considering quitting altogether. But one night after visiting, Adam asked about the book, and I shared how I felt. He just looked at me and said I couldn't quit. He said he'd help however I needed him to and that he thought I should reach out to some literary agents again. So I reluctantly agreed, thinking I probably wouldn't do much of anything.

The next day, Adam messaged, called, and texted me to make sure I had made the calls and sent the emails to agents. This guy was the best accountability partner I'd ever had.

This time I got a meeting and was asked to submit a proposal. I figured that now that the hard part was done, Adam would split. He'd done his good deed, and I was grateful. But instead, he helped me shape my book proposal and encouraged me along the way. He was one of the first calls I made after I got a book deal (Jodi was first), and he has been one of my greatest cheerleaders.

I'm not sure he knows it, but he changed my life. Not just with the book deal and encouragement but by loving me well when I had no idea what loving well means or how to believe in love, trust in love, invest in it. But I now understand that we all need someone like Adam and that once we've experienced love, one of the most rewarding things we can do is to be the kind of person Adam is for someone else. It doesn't have to be complicated or result in a book deal. It just requires being there to offer what you can and cheer them along the way.

An exercise I do with clients is to have them stand behind an empty chair to help them visualize a person sitting there and then ask them to talk about someone who has loved them well. Who is their model of love? You'd probably guess that grandmas, grandpas, mothers, and fathers often are chosen. But there's an even more popular answer.

Pets. Dogs and cats.

I think this happens because pets love us the way people in our lives should love us but often don't.

Pets, eager to spend time with us, are usually happy to see us when we arrive home and are often great at comforting us when we are hurting. Although we can't communicate much with them, they seem to have an understanding that goes deeper than words.

Maybe you've experienced this before with a pet. My pet was Nikita, a Brittany springer spaniel that I helped raise to be a hunting dog for a man my mom dated shortly after my parents divorced.

Nikita didn't know it, but she was brought into a chaotic environment, and although it was my job to take care of her as a puppy, mostly she took care of me. We had an understanding. Both of us wanted to run away. Nikita because she was a puppy who loved to run, and I because I wanted a different life. We were stuck where we were, but at least it was together.

Although Nikita ran away a lot, she always came back. The first couple of times she jumped the fence, I sprinted after her, yelling and begging her to return, which she did. But after a while, whenever she'd escape, she seemed to think better of it. I'd look outside and see her jump back over the fence and come up the steps to the house. I'd open the door and she'd just look at me with big eyes that seemed to say, "We can't really run away, can we, Jason?"

I learned from Nikita that although we still get the urge to run sometimes, there are always people in our lives worth running back to. And I decided I wanted to learn to be one of those people.

Who has loved you well? Maybe it was a caregiver, friend, romantic partner, or pet. Why did you identify them? What attributes of their love for you felt special, different from other people? What might that person or pet want you to know in the midst of what you are working through? Would they be cheering you on and offering encouragement?

Chapter 13

IT'S NOT ABOUT PERFECTION

What is love supposed to be like? Should it look like the love we read about in a romance novel? Like something out of a Hallmark movie? Or maybe like drowning in an icy sea so that your partner might live or leaving everything to run to someone or maybe even being with someone who costs you everything? Is it messy, loud, and chaotic? Which version of love is correct?

For some of us, this is a tough question to answer. As we've discussed, sometimes our ideas of love go back to a poor childhood example. When this is the case, we're often able to recognize that the love we were shown is unhealthy, but we struggle with knowing what healthy love is supposed to look like.

What's more, love isn't one size fits all. Love looks different based on our personalities, experiences, preferences, and more. Because of this, it's sometimes easier to describe what love isn't.

Love isn't perfect, nor does it need perfection in order to exist.

Who has impacted you the most in life? I mean the people

who have acted as a rudder, guiding and directing you, whether in spoken or unspoken ways. For most of us, these individuals are not showy. They're not people who've made any grand gestures or performed for us or entertained us in a certain way. Instead, they are people who simply cared. Maybe they didn't set out to play this big role in our lives, but they did so nonetheless.

I can name two people like this in my life: Peg and Annette. These two individuals had a huge impact on me. When Jodi and I first got married, we struggled significantly. I say "significantly" because we had gotten to a point where we didn't know whether we should be married any longer. This was in large part because of my behavior. Marriage was starting to feel to me like a new set of shackles. In my opinion, I had already been shackled for a very long time before marriage, and now needed to quickly find freedom. Marriage seemed like the opposite of freedom, so I often questioned it.

This was a particularly painful time for Jodi, and it led her to reach out to a church. At the church, we met with two counseling students, Peg and Annette, who were many years older than we were. Both were in a program that taught them how to act as mentors and coaches, in line with biblical teaching, to couples who were struggling. At the time, I still had a major beef with God, and so the idea of working with students in a program with a biblical focus at a church seemed like the setup for a terrible ending to our marriage. I reluctantly agreed to meet with them but had mostly written off the whole process before we even started.

Our first meeting at the church happened in the middle of the summer, the day the air-conditioning went out. Or at least it felt like the air-conditioning went out, given how much I sweat that afternoon. At that first meeting, both Peg and Annette seemed nervous. Later I learned that this was their first time meeting with a couple. And although it was their first time, they were able to listen. In addition to listening, they made a genuine attempt to help us. I left that day feeling strangely better, despite still believing I couldn't trust or count on these people that we'd hired.

We ended up meeting with Peg and Annette at the church again, but also in a hotel and occasionally at a park, to work on our marriage. All those meetings changed me, and eventually our marriage was transformed. The surprising thing is that I don't think the transformation occurred because Peg and Annette were such wonderful therapists. I'm certain they are talented at helping people, but that's not what changed me. What changed me was that for the first time in my life, someone listened to me. They listened and tried to help. Jodi, of course, listened to me and loved me—that's why I married her. But besides her, the list of people who had listened to me and had my best interests at heart was very short. And now these people, complete strangers to me, did something I'd searched my entire life to find. And they did it without asking for anything in return.

Although I didn't know it then, Peg and Annette made such a significant impact on my life because they taught me that it was okay to trust people, that there were people out there who would listen and wanted to help. It was so simple: I just needed someone to listen. In those moments with Peg and Annette, God was present. Little needed to be said in an elegant way, no big therapeutic intervention needed to happen—I just needed love. The presence of love and acceptance and awareness shaped my life. I learned that the people who help me most might not show up the way I expect them to, and that the people who help me the most might be the ones I unfairly discount or look down on. They were the first to line up to give me free therapy when no one else would. They have stayed in contact with me over the years, congratulating me every time I've had success and being present in my life. They have given me so much.

So often we look at our lives in terms of packaging and expectation. Some places are fun to shop because of the packages that things come in. But just because something's packaged well doesn't mean it's what we need. But that's easy to forget. As I go forward in my life, I want to remember Peg and Annette not for all the things I expected them to be but for the unexpected ways they were loving and kind and authentic, the ways that made all the difference.

Love is not meant to be perfect. We're not perfect, so how could love be? That's not to say love can't, and shouldn't, be healthy, but it's not good for us or the people around us when we strive for perfection in love, because that's often a reflection of our woundedness around love.

It seems counterintuitive, but love that never faces challenges, is messy, or has conflict is pretty unfulfilling. Although we might hope to find someone who does exactly what we want all the time, that would be boring. When we see really messy examples of imperfect love, it can lead us to think that healthy love is just the opposite. But the healthy love most of us want and need is messy at times.

Peg and Annette showed me that love doesn't need to be perfect to be meaningful. The only kind of love I needed in that season, in order to love Jodi better, was a love that listened. I didn't need a bunch of advice or tips, I just needed someone who would listen to me, and Peg and Annette did just that.

Love isn't always perfect.

And that's perfectly okay.

> Take a couple of minutes to write down what you have been taught about love. Do you think it should look this way? Now write down what you think love should look like. Is this how your relationships look today, or do you need to make some adjustments?

Chapter 14

LOVE SHOULDN'T BE A SECRET

Have you ever been surprised that someone sent you a message or told you they care about you? Most of us have probably been there at one time or another—otherwise unaware that another person cares for us because we're distracted or caught up in our own heads.

I'm reminded of a time in middle school when we did a Secret Santa gift exchange. Like most of the other kids in my class, I was not thrilled that we were doing this. I had just gotten my braces on, and my mother had somehow talked me into wearing my headgear to school for a couple of days, and that look made a lasting impact on my fellow classmates. Suffice it to say, I was not feeling lovable at that time.

We all drew names, and then the day came to hand out our gifts. I gave my gift without really thinking too much about it. I couldn't even tell you what it was. But when it was my turn to receive a gift, a girl in my class gave me a CD and a handmade card. In the card she said that she admired my willingness to be myself and be nice to people. I was shocked. CDs were pretty expensive back then, and I could not believe someone had noticed me like that.

I had all kinds of reasons why a person wouldn't care about me, and this thoughtful gift flew in the face of all of them.

I was unlovable because I had braces.

I was unlovable because my parents were divorced.

I was unlovable because bad things happened to me, and bad things happened to me because I was unlovable.

Maybe you can relate?

And yet someone saw through all the things that I thought made me unlovable and loved me anyway. What I admired most about the girl who was my Secret Santa was her willingness to risk saying something.

Sometimes we think telling someone we love them has to be this huge undertaking like renting a plane to write out our feelings in the sky or buying some unbelievably expensive piece of jewelry.

But that's really not necessary. Expressing love to someone, whether romantic or platonic, can just as effectively be done in little ways that are often far more meaningful.

Sending a friend an encouraging text.

Telling someone that their actions made your day.

Giving someone understanding and listening to them when they need someone to talk to.

The thing is, telling someone you love them, whether in a big or small way, requires some vulnerability, which can be scary. Perhaps we once told a parent or someone important to us that we loved them, and we felt like that love was unreciprocated. This left us wounded and fearful of ever trying again with someone else.

I understand. It's scary to tell someone you love them. So many love stories focus on one person sharing their love for another at great risk to their safety. It's daring and heroic. While I think this makes for a great story, I don't think it's typical, outside of movies and books.

Instead, admitting you love someone often looks like admiring a potential friend but being afraid to say something.

Wanting to ask someone out but being too scared to do so.

Loving a family member but not saying anything.

We sometimes don't say anything, and then we regret it, maybe even for a lifetime.

Death has a way of reminding us of unexpressed love. Since getting married, I always had a close relationship with Grandma Phyllis. Grandma Phyllis was my wife's paternal grandma. She and I hit it off from the beginning.

Phyllis had a difficult childhood that caused her to leave home and get married at a young age. Even as a teen she had already witnessed significant loss, trauma, and death. But she started a family with the idea that she could make something better for herself. And she did. It was not without lots of hurdles, but Phyllis changed the trajectory of her life from that of victim to survivor.

Phyllis enjoyed baking, fishing, and a game called pinochle. She was also a pretty good dancer and one of the best hosts and lovers of people I have ever known. She was never the main event but was always standing to the side waiting to help and cheering others on.

Having lost most of my grandparents early on in life, I hadn't had a close relationship with a grandparent for a long time. I wasn't sure whether we were supposed to eat Werther's Original Caramels and sit in La-Z-Boy recliners watching old television shows or how this relationship was supposed to go. But none of that really mattered. Phyllis was just there.

She'd send me cards for every holiday and give me gift cards that I know took her a long time to save up for. She'd bake me and my family treats and do things like go fishing with us. She was just an amazing person who had a beautiful story. And then one day she passed away.

She didn't leave in a dramatic or drawn-out way, she was just called home to be with the Lord one afternoon while having a meal with her two sons and my mother-in-law. Her passing was as Phyllis as anything could be: not a lot of to-do or discussion, and everything that needed to be prepared had already been done. One day she was just gone.

And it broke my heart.

Because the thing is, somewhere along the line I had subconsciously decided that Phyllis would have to live forever. She would just know how much I cared about her or how I couldn't have a birthday without the angel food cake she made that we both loved. She must have known that when I needed someone the most, just knowing that she would be there in her quiet way was comforting to me.

But what if she didn't know? I hope and suspect she did know how much I loved her, but I wasn't good at telling her. I spent a lot more time eating her cakes than sending her cards. I just assumed she had to know. And now, years later, I find myself wondering whether she knew how highly I regarded her.

Did she know how important she was in my life or that her life was an inspiration to me?

Maybe you have your own Grandma Phyllis who has loved you well over the years. Or maybe you have a spouse who has been there through thick and thin. Maybe it's even just a person on the periphery of your life, like a barista or mail carrier, who brightens your day.

Please don't let your feelings go unsaid, even if it feels easier in the moment not to. You see, for most of us the idea of laying our feelings out there for the world to know feels incredibly risky, even if it's a pretty sure bet that the other person feels the same way.

Maybe you've seen the videos online where one person professes their love for the other at a sporting event or at Disneyworld or some other place that's full of people, and they are met, at best, with nothing or, at worst, openly rejected. Like you, I usually cringe for these people who bared their hearts only to be left hanging or rejected, but I've changed how I look at these situations.

What I've learned is that some people will love you and others won't, but that's okay. (Being a people pleaser, I can hardly type this.) And even more than being okay, it's helpful to know where you stand, because sometimes we aren't sure or are very bad mind-readers who could use some direction. And so in an odd way, I've stopped feeling so afraid to share how I feel because I want to know where I stand.

The thing is that as children, sharing our love for someone and being rejected can be the difference between life and death. If your parents don't love you, then who will care for you, feed you, and do parenting stuff? It's a terrifying thought as a kid, and sometimes we carry this fear into adulthood, imagining that we are risking just as much telling someone how we feel about them as adults. But here's the reality. You aren't a kid anymore. You survived your childhood and are resilient. As much as the prospect seems terrifying today, the reality is that the stakes have probably changed. The other person doesn't have to feel the way you feel. You can even love someone who feels differently about you. Today it's okay.

So don't let love be a secret. Life is so short, and we don't often get told which interaction we have with someone is the last one. Instead, life happens quickly, and if we aren't intentional, we may miss our chance and be left with questions and even regret.

If you love someone, tell them or show them. If you've been hurt before, start small. But know that telling someone might make all the difference.

Think about who you might need to check in with. Who might benefit from hearing how you feel about them? Now think of how you might go about telling them. Remember that it does not have to be a grand gesture. Instead, start small and build from there.

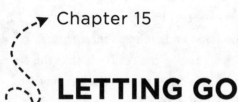

Chapter 15

LETTING GO

I absolutely love to Tenkara fish. Tenkara is fishing with a telescoping pole that has a line attached to a simple hook. Because the hook has no barbs, it can be more difficult to catch fish, and not every fish that bites gets caught. When the fish do get caught and you pull them in, the hook allows you to release them without significant harm. It's beautiful. You can briefly hold the fish and admire it before letting it go back into the water and back to its life. Other fishing hooks are better at catching fish, but they also tend to injure or kill a fish when you take it off the hook, which is what makes Tenkara amazing.

I think God calls us to be more like the Tenkara hook than the one with all the barbs. We ought to catch and release people in a caring and beautiful way, allowing them to come back if they want to. Otherwise, we tend to snag them and fight to hold on, injuring or damaging the people we love. It makes sense that we do life this way, though. We want and need people, and it's hard to let go sometimes. That's okay. Although I would like to hold on to every fish I catch, I know I cannot. (Also, Jodi is seriously not into my keeping a bunch of trout in the house.)

Love ebbs and flows. This is difficult to reconcile with,

because many of us yearn for a consistent and unchanging love, one that we may never have received from our parents. But the truth of the matter is, we can't control love, because love involves real people and real problems, and, as you've probably experienced for yourself once or twice, we can't control people. The harder we try to hold on to them, the more often we lose them.

I think of Jesus' crucifixion here. Had I been there with Jesus, I know I wouldn't have wanted him to go through dying on the cross. I like to believe that I would have done anything to stop it. But that was not to be and would not have been for me to control anyway.

When we try to control love, we suffocate it.

Maybe our control comes out as jealousy.

Maybe it looks like overfunctioning.

Or maybe it looks like giving up well before we need to because that feels safer than taking a risk. Everyone wants to be in love. No one wants to think about what it's like to lose love.

There may be people in your life you are holding on to too tightly whom you need to let go. Maybe it's time to give letting go a shot.

A good friend of mine talks about how if we ball our hand up into a fist, eventually when we open our hand, it doesn't open as far. He uses this illustration to talk about how holding too tightly not only gets in the way of love but also causes us pain and limits the love we might give.

When I think of holding on too tightly, I can't help but think of when I was a kid and my dad took us boating. I didn't get much time with my dad growing up, and so that alone made it a big deal. On top of the boating, he excused my brother and me from school, saying we were sick. That made it a day to remember. My brother, my dad, my dad's friend, and I drove to the lake grinning from ear to ear.

Eventually, we got the boat on the water and hooked up the tube behind it for some good old-fashioned tubing. I did not then and still cannot now understand how anyone can see tubing as a good idea, and I have the chiropractor bills to prove it!

Nonetheless, we all took our turn on the tube. My younger brother went first, and after a couple of sharp turns and hitting a few waves, he flew off like a seventy-pound sack of potatoes. I was up next and managed to stay on longer, mostly out of a competitive spirit and lack of care for my lower back. But eventually, like my brother, I hit a wave and went skimming over the water.

Next up was my dad's friend, and it was clear that he had the most resolve to hang on out of all of us. After a time, my dad accelerated the boat, but still his friend hung on. The faster we went, the more I cringed every time we hit a wave, wondering how long he could stay on the tube. Eventually my dad decided to give it all he had, opened up the engine, and began weaving across the water so his friend would hit the biggest waves possible.

It was amazing! It was terrible! My Snickers bar flew out of the boat. My brother and I hung on for dear life, but as my dad's friend hit every wave, as painful as it looked, he just kept hanging on and getting flung around like a rag doll.

Finally I think I yelled that he should just let go. He had held on long enough. We were impressed, after all. And then came the wave. Another boat had been driving nearby and putting out an equally impressive wake. As the two wakes merged, Dad's friend hit them head on. Have you ever seen a slinky that deviates from its path and tumbles erratically down the stairs before clanging to a stop at the bottom? That's what we watched my dad's friend do on the tube, and to be honest it was a bit tough to see.

We circled back to pick him up, and as he came out of the water, he was rattled, but smiling. I might have thought everything was fine if I hadn't noticed that there was a bit of an interruption in his smile. He was missing one of his front teeth. Now, I'm no dentist, and so I don't want to talk out of turn, but this seemed like kind of a big deal.

I remember that as he got into the boat, I said to him a couple of times, "Why didn't you just let go?" It seemed so pointless to hang on for so long.

But what my dad's friend said next has stayed with me. He replied, "It just seemed like I should hang on, and the waves didn't seem so bad from where I was."

So many times in my life, I or people I care about have hung on for way longer than we should have, only to get hurt. Sometimes we are just too close to the waves to see the danger others see. It's terribly important to have a trusted group of friends and a community to help us see when it's time to let go and to be willing to be influenced by their advice.

To be clear, I'm not advising you to pick up the phone and quit all kinds of relationships, but I am asking you to consider whether you are holding on too tightly or for far longer than you should. If the answer is unclear, it's okay to talk to a trusted friend or professional to gain some clarity. Just know that you don't have to hold on until you lose a tooth. There is no award for who can hold on the longest, and your dentist most certainly would not advise riding it out until you're missing part of your smile.

We can't control love like that. Sometimes we have to trust love enough to know it'll come back to us if it's right, and other times we need to let go when we know it's not serving us or the other person. It's a hard truth to learn, but it's one we, and the people around us, will be better off for if we make it part of our lives and relationships.

Almost every time that I do a question-and-answer segment online or with a live audience, I get asked how to know when it's time to let go of a friend, romantic partner, or spouse. I suspect the motivation for the question is "I'm hurting and feeling stuck. I don't think I can hold on much longer. What can I do?"

This is such an important question and one that my dad's friend might have been asking before losing that tooth. The trouble is that we often ask ourselves this question many times over before asking someone who can see the situation more clearly. And in this way, we can suffer much longer than we need to and sometimes for someone who isn't even asking us to hold on.

So I usually respond by asking, "Does the person know that you are about to let go?" And the interesting thing is that almost every single time, the questioner responds yes. Often they say that they have told the person many times, but the other person seems unphased, uncommitted, or unresponsive, which is what is causing the questioner so much strife. I usually point out that most people who ask this question already know the answer but are hoping someone else will say it.

When I'm standing in the middle of a river having just caught a trout, it's easy to see that it harms the fish to pull it around by the hook. And so I am always quick to take the hook out and put the fish back into the water, because I can see how much it hurts it to be hooked, and I also know how much work it is for me to hold it there. It's just not sustainable or healthy for either of us.

So I put the fish back into the water so that it can live, and I watch to see where it wants to go. Sometimes the fish is gone so fast that I can hardly catch a glimpse before it's gone, while other times it will swim in my vicinity for a long time. I love these times mostly because it doesn't require much more effort than showing up to where the fish lives and giving it an opportunity to stay.

I'm not comparing your past, your boyfriend or girlfriend, your parent, or your coworker to a trout. Really. But the premise is the same. Lasting relationships are about meeting someone where you are and inviting them to show up. You can't force them, and you must be there to do the inviting. Sometimes you don't spend a long time in that place or can't sustain the invitation, and the reason is usually less about the other person and more about your circumstances, but you know when you have to go or when they've already left. And it's at that point, when the water gets too cold or the trout has swum away, that you load up your things and go somewhere else. It doesn't mean that you won't see them again or that you can't come back to the spot and try again, but it means that you're done for now. You can always invite them another time if you want.

Take a couple of minutes to reflect on this chapter. Do you tend to be the person who drops the line too quickly in love and relationships, or do you keep hanging on even when people are yelling at you to let go? Do you need to consider letting go of things in your past or of a relationship in the present? If so, who can you talk with about those situations?

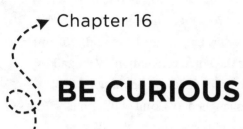

Chapter 16

BE CURIOUS

I went to a conference for mental-health counselors some time ago, and the conference was held in an expo/auditorium-type building where there was also, unbeknownst to me, a horse convention happening at the same time.

Yes, you read that right. I live in the Midwest, so a convention all about horses isn't super unusual.

I was trying to find the right room for the first session of the mental-health conference, and I was struggling a little bit to locate it. Eventually, I walked into a pretty crowded auditorium, thinking this must be the right place, since so many people were there. As everyone sat down, I took my seat and listened to the speaker start his talk. Initially he was talking about the brain and neuroscience. This was an area of interest to me, but not my strong suit, so I eagerly listened, uncertain of some of the terms he was using and references he was making. During this whole first part of the talk, I was also unaware that nearly everyone around me was dressed in country-and-western apparel. I was just excited to be there and learn from these cowboy counselors.

Well, probably twenty minutes went by and I was getting more and more confused by the terms this speaker was using and the references he kept pointing to. Eventually someone in the auditorium raised her hand and asked, "Is this the mental-health-counseling session?" To which the person next to her (who was sporting a huge cowboy hat) laughed and said, "No, this is the session on horses for the horse convention. We're talking about the neuroscience and brain development of horses."

Everyone in the session laughed. It's kind of hilarious when you think about it, because right after the cowboy-hat guy said this was a horse session, about twenty people stood up and walked toward the exit because they were in the wrong room. I was one of them.

What's fascinating to me about this situation is that out of the twenty people who were in the wrong room, only one asked the question. The rest of us just sat there, feeling like we were in the wrong spot, unsure, but rather than say anything, we just sat through the talk.

We do this same thing in life sometimes. Our gut tells us something's not right, tells us we must reach out or ask for help or say something, but we don't. Instead we sit through the horse seminar. Now, in the horse people's defense, it was a very lovely seminar, and I appreciated their sharing about the neuroscience of horses, but I ended up missing the part of the conference I had really wanted to go to.

Instead of hearing about a specific topic at this conference, I wasted some of the limited time I had that day hearing about horses. I wasn't curious enough about the feelings I was having in the horse seminar to understand that things were kind of off in that auditorium. *Why is that guy wearing a cowboy hat? Why don't I recognize any of the terms the speaker is using?* That lack of curiosity caused me to miss the topic I was actually interested in and the people I shared a mutual interest with (though I do own a pair of cowboy boots). What's more is that my preconceived notions about how things would look blocked my curiosity. I've learned the hard way that sometimes how we expect things to be overshadows how they actually are.

In 2018 a story spread quickly around the internet about a family who had purchased a puppy they had expected to grow into a large dog (Tibetan mastiff). They were filled with excitement about this new addition to their family. They fed it, played with it, loved it, and made it part of their home.

The puppy began to grow. Not surprising. But the puppy grew a little too much. The family continued to be surprised by how big the puppy was getting and how much food it was consuming. Each day, they fed it and it always wanted more. This was alarming, but the family believed that they had simply gotten the largest puppy in the litter and that soon it would quit growing. This continued for two years.

It was when the owners noticed that the dog had surpassed by more than seventy pounds what it was expected to weigh, paired with the fact that it ate several pounds of food each day, that they wondered what was going on. After contacting authorities, the family learned that the puppy they had purchased some two years ago was actually an endangered Asiatic black bear. This changed everything, and the bear that had lived as a dog was soon transported to a rescue center where it could be taken care of appropriately.

Can you imagine raising what you think is a puppy only to

find out some two years later that it's a bear? That instead of a fluffy family pet, you are raising an animal that could hurt you or destroy your home? Sounds unbelievable, doesn't it?

When asked why the family kept the dog so long, they responded that they had expected it to be a Tibetan mastiff because that's what they were told it was when they purchased it in a market. As it got bigger and bigger, it became harder to believe, but in many ways the dog looked similar to the bear, and so it took a long time to start asking some very important questions.

Maybe you are thinking you would have made the connection much sooner or at least asked some questions. But would you have?

I'm not so sure I would have. I think I would have believed what I was told to expect until it was no longer believable. It's human nature to believe what we are told and to set our expectations accordingly.

It happens a lot in childhood, friendships, and romantic relationships: we sign up for a puppy and set expectations that prevent us from being curious and sometimes end up learning that we raised a bear instead.

A lack of curiosity doesn't always lead us to raise a bear, though. Sometimes it gets in the way of taking good care of something or someone that is truly wonderful but labeled incorrectly. And while we continue to treat ourselves or someone else in accordance with what we were told or expected, we later find out that had we asked some questions, things might have been different. We might have been happier, felt more loved, kept a relationship that was important to us.

In my mind, one of the best parts of becoming a therapist is decorating your office for the first time. Although my first office was small, it was mine, and it signaled that I had finally done it. I had made it through school and an internship and now was ready to start off my new career. As part of that, I was given a plant by a friend. Although this seemed like a nice gesture, it was also a responsibility that I quickly skirted, and this new plant began to wither.

To this day, if you asked me what kind of plant it was, I couldn't tell you or would probably just guess that it was a fern. All I know is that like all plants, it needed water, and I wasn't great at watering it. After some reminders from Jodi, I started to water it and eventually it perked back up. One day when I was talking with a client, I looked over and noticed something amazing. The plant had suddenly sprouted the most beautiful orange flower. I was so shocked that I called my friend and told them the good news, to which they replied, "I thought it was a fern too!" After some research we learned that the plant had been put in the wrong pot at the store, and that, if taken care of, it would grow into a beautiful flowering plant.

You probably see where I'm going with this. Some of us have been planted in the wrong pots. We may have been told that we were just a fern when instead we were something far more beautiful, but we'd never know it if we never asked.

This isn't a chapter about not trusting anyone at any time, or about horse conventions, bears, or plants. It's a reminder that life isn't always what we expect it to be or what we are told it should look like. Sometimes it's far worse, but sometimes it is so very much better. The trick is asking some questions when they arise so that at the very least we know what we are dealing with. Because sometimes we are feeding bears that will grow up to walk on their hind legs and scare the ever-loving wits out of us, but other times we, or relationships we are in, are so much more than we could have ever imagined.

It takes some courage to ask questions, so start in a safe place with people who are likely to give you a truthful answer. Not everyone is invested in our curiosity and in pointing us in the right direction.

If you are a person of faith, know there is always one place you can go to get the truth. God will never mislead, lie to, or betray you, so if you are looking for a place to start asking some big questions, such as "Am I worthy of love?" or "Am I as bad as I think I am?" prayer is an excellent place to begin, because God will meet you with both grace and truth.

> Is there a question you have been wondering about? Maybe it's a question about who you are, your worth, or someone in your life. Take a moment to identify that question and who would be a safe person to ask. If you can't think of anyone, look for who might be able to point you in the right direction. Or maybe God is the one you need to ask. What one small step could you take toward asking what needs to be asked and gaining some clarity?

Chapter 17

CONSISTENCY WINS

One of the times I felt the most connected to other people was in high school. I had a solid group of friends. We would hang out almost every day and ride to and from school together. Our favorite thing to do was to go to a gas station and get blue cream sodas and salted nut rolls. And yes, I've always had the junk food preferences of a sixty-year-old man. But anyway, we loved driving to the gas station and talking about how life was going.

To connect, we must have something to connect over, shared experiences. And it's vitally important as we develop connection that we share those experiences consistently. Consistency wins, every time. Even though school wasn't always my favorite thing, it allowed me to connect consistently with my friends. Without that, and the blue cream soda (which I think had like seventy grams of sugar per bottle), I never would have had the friends I did in high school. Consistency really gives relationships time to thrive. It's like fertilizer for your relationships.

I remember those days so fondly because doing things together was required. Only one of us had a car, so we needed the other guys to get anywhere after school. But as adults, that's such a struggle. We don't need to rely on other people as much as we used to and aren't forced to interact with people as much as we were in high school or college. Instead, we need to look for something to consistently connect with people around so relationships can grow.

One of the best ways to develop consistency is to have a system for when you don't feel like connecting. Because let's face it, you won't always want to work to be connected. Even though the blue cream soda was delicious, a person can drink only so much of it. It's in these times that we need a system if we want to stay connected and keep our relationships moving forward.

What does that system look like? Maybe it's putting on your Google calendar a recurring dinner with friends or an every-other-Friday date with your spouse or a weekend once a month to go out of town to see your in-laws.

Connection doesn't have to be complicated, but it does need to be consistent or it doesn't happen.

But what about when you don't want to? Like really don't? What about when you don't want to do it anymore?

If you're anything like me, you'll often start doing something with the greatest of intentions, only for those intentions to fizzle out thanks to frustration or boredom. Many of us find ourselves in this situation when trying to recover from something. It's easy to pursue recovery in the middle of the crisis, but when the dust settles and life returns to "normal," continuing to work on ourselves seems a lot less exciting and we often quit well before the project is done.

This temptation to quit when things get tough reminds me of the time I hired a contractor to finish my basement a few years ago. We lived in a small home and the contractor agreed to singlehandedly finish the lower level of our house for us. Everything started off well enough. He had a great attitude and seemed excited about the job, and Jodi even made him cookies. A couple of weeks in, though, things started to get shaky. There was less whistling, more leaving early, and I'm pretty sure I heard crying in the bathroom at one point.

After several weeks, the basement was nearly done, so one night I went downstairs to check in with him. He showed me each completed room before we walked into the still unfinished living room. While I was busy looking around, he sat down on an overturned bucket, looked at me, and said, "This really isn't fun anymore. My friends invited me to a concert, and I'd much rather go to that." At that moment, what was left was the messy stuff: the paint that was splattered all over the floor and trim work, the drywall dust covering everything, the plastic taped to the windows. If you made a list of the things you didn't want to do, that is what was left.

Although I understood his feelings, I was pretty shocked when he put away his things and headed off to the concert, not to return for several days. I was mad. (Maybe that's an understatement.) The job wasn't finished, and he quit because it was no longer fun? I couldn't believe how ridiculous he was being, so I withheld payment until the job was complete. After a couple of days, he must have realized he needed the money, because he came back and finished the job.

Can you relate to this scenario? How many times have we pursued the process of healing when it was "fun" or there was a crisis only to leave the hard work undone the minute something better came along? How often do we leave only to be brought back to the unfinished basement when life gets hard? Although I was really ticked off about the situation, this contractor taught me an important lesson: the job isn't over until it's done. Regardless of whether it's fun, we cannot leave the job half done or the recovery half finished. If we do, we'll have to return later when people (or ourselves) are even more ticked off because we've failed to finish what we started.

I totally get it. There are points in the growth process where it seems easier to stop or to return to where we came from. Some of the times I've felt like this are when I've:

- Moved to a new city
- Started a new job
- Ended a relationship
- Worked hard to get in shape but saw little progress after months of work

Sometimes we get far enough from the feelings, grief, or brokenness we are working on that we forget how bad it was when we left, and all we want to do is return to what we know. There's no shame in feeling this way. The shame comes when we return to our old ways of being, feeling, and thinking, knowing that we should have kept moving forward. And if you return enough times, it becomes harder to leave again and easier to accept a bad situation or the pain.

I'm reminded of my time working with people who were just

released from prison. I realized early on that many of them had an unbelievable ability to make a fresh start. They would walk out of the prison gates with nothing to their name but what they had in their pockets and, in only a month or two, would create an entire life. I was always amazed because I think I would be too terrified to do such a thing. But although they were masterful at starting over, what some of them struggled with the most was creating a sustainable life. I think this is because of trauma, a lack of good role models, mental illness, sin, lots of things, but this lack of know-how prevented them from staying put in their new lives. Often an inmate would secure a job, find an apartment, and then begin dating someone new. They would be on top of the world. Having just gotten out of prison, it appeared that things were going to be different now and they had hope. But slowly, conflicts would arise at work and at home. And while many of them were normal conflicts in most people's lives, the person would be unsure how to deal with them in a healthy way. Rather than return to bad habits, some of the men would try to stomach the problems and push down their emotions in a sincere effort to maintain their new lives. But eventually the problems would get too big and the person's emotions would boil over and lead them back to self-destructive behaviors like addiction, crime, or impulsivity. It was hard to watch because I was really cheering for them to succeed, but I could also relate to their doing their best to build something new but lacking the tools to sustain it.

Imagine building a house and never paying for upkeep or the utilities. Although you have a home, your house would start to deteriorate and eventually you'd be left with nothing. While it seems simple enough, many of us struggle to pay the utilities and keep up with the maintenance our lives require, not usually because we don't want to but often because we don't know how to or haven't been shown how.

If you feel disconnected after reading this, realize that not only do you need to do the work to get connected but you need to keep doing it. I promise that you will be glad you did. When you feel that going to therapy, talking about your difficulties, or whatever healing process you are in is no longer fun and you want to quit, the best thing to do is to remember why you started to do the work in the first place: to find connection.

How are you doing at making a consistent effort to stay connected? Is there something that you could be doing more often to help you be more connected? What is it?

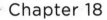
Chapter 18

NO MORE ISOLATION

I had a friend in high school who played on the varsity football team as a freshman. Although he was very talented, he was younger and skinnier than the rest of the team. This became even more apparent when he would get tackled and thrown across the field like a rag doll. After watching him get tackled mercilessly during one of his games, I asked him what it was like to be a freshman varsity football player. Although I thought it was awesome that he was on the team, I guess I also wondered why he subjected himself to such pain and difficulty. I half expected him to tell me that it was terrible, but he surprised me by saying that although he barely filled out his football jersey, at least he was on the team. He then looked at me with grass sticking out of his helmet and said, "It's okay, I'll grow into it." And he did. He came back the next year bigger and wiser, and the year after that even more so. My friend became a force to be reckoned with on the field and a player people respected immensely.

Life is like that sometimes. God puts us on a team of people who are more advanced or successful than us and we are tempted to quit because we don't quite fill out the jersey yet.

If we aren't careful, we forget that most of the people we look up to didn't fill out their jerseys when they started either. Some were most certainly smaller than us but stuck with it anyway. I think of how God signed David up for the varsity team and how that led to his defeating Goliath because he didn't quit and just ran with it.

Learning how to connect well with others can be a lot like getting a jersey that doesn't quite fit yet. It can seem at times that everyone else knows how to have healthier, better, more rewarding relationships while we are stuck on the sidelines just trying to figure out how to play the game. We feel alone and unworthy rather than encouraged to get out there to form new relationships or strengthen existing ones. Sometimes it seems like we aren't cut out for connection, but if we aren't careful, this can become a powerful message in our lives.

One of the most difficult things I've had to realize as a counselor is that although counseling is important, sometimes the same result can be achieved in a far simpler manner. I'm not trying to dissuade anyone from working with a counselor. I'm just trying to call attention to something important: loneliness. Sometimes the clients I see are profoundly disconnected and isolated. In our world today, this is probably the norm rather than the exception. Although we should be more connected now than ever, we aren't, and that's not okay.

If you look at yourself and think, *I have few to no friends and there isn't really anyone I can talk to about the important things in my life*, this applies to you, and we need to change that, because friends are a heck of a lot cheaper than therapy and they're usually more fun, although there is room for both.

But how does someone find their "team" of friends? It's not always easy.

It's important to just have friends you can talk to and relate to. We need to have information coming in to challenge us, to grow us, to help us discern who we are. Many of us are missing that type of community, or we're trading it in for something far less valuable. Rather than have friends to whom we can say, "I got into a fight with my wife yesterday. Can I talk to you about that?" we opt for online likes and comments. We all need authentic relationships that allow us to call one another and say, "I'm struggling with something. Can we talk about it?" or, "I experienced a big success yesterday. Can I tell you more?"

You don't have to settle for shallow friendships. And if you are settling, that could be why you feel the way you do.

Many social media platforms out there today tell us that they're going to offer us something similar to this community. But that's nonsense. Social media is about projecting who you are and seeing whether other people like it. Authentic connection is sharing who you are and receiving acceptance. This is not the same as sharing what you ate for dinner or your latest vacation pictures. Real connection is vulnerably sharing who you are. You do that with people who are safe, who are qualified to hear, and who can help, not with hundreds of people on the internet whom you sort of know. If you build relationships authentically, your need for therapy is probably going to go down quite a bit. I don't mean to diss therapy, but a lot of what my colleagues and I do as therapists is help people to realize things about themselves that could have been shown to them by a group of trusted and healthy friends.

Now, maybe you're thinking, *Hey, Jason, I hear you, but I don't know how to make friends.* I get that. Making friends may be a skill you need to work on, and there are people who can help you with that. You must work at creating outlets for authentic and vulnerable connection, because social media connections are not enough. Social media has many benefits, but it dissuades us from having the authentic connections we need. I know if I have a fight with my wife, that's probably not going to be my Facebook status.

As connected as we are online, you would think that we would also have that community in real life. But often we don't. I want to challenge you to look at your life and ask, "Do I have three people whom I trust, who are safe, and whom I deem to be healthy whom I could call if I had a problem? People whom I could tell honestly what happened and they would give me feedback?" If you don't, begin to work on that today. You can work on that by finding ways to connect with others through hobbies and interests or through your faith. If you don't have that kind of community, you're not experiencing the fullness of what God created us to enjoy on this earth: community and connection to others.

Back to the football story: what if we do have that community, that team, but we don't feel like we fit in? What if we can't seem to fill out the jersey? What do we do when everyone else is already good at football and we're just the skinny freshman trying not to get laid out all the time? For example:

- Everyone in your friend group seems to be farther along in their faith than you are.
- Everyone you know is part of one political party and you identify more with another.
- Your friends have all been in their jobs for years, while you just switched careers and are learning the ropes at a new job.
- Everyone else is either single or married and you're the opposite.
- Everyone either has kids or doesn't have kids and you're on the other end.

The list could go on. My point is your community looks more like the upperclassmen on the football team while you're still a freshman. It's tempting to think that others will never understand where you're coming from or that you'll never be able to get to where they are.

When we find ourselves in a group like this, which might be a community group, a professional organization, a church group, or a new group of friends, when our experiences or views don't line up with those around us, it can be tempting to quit. *I'm already the smallest person on the team, why would I stick around when everyone views the playbook so much differently than I do?* But that's when learning how to connect and to work on connection is most important.

Don't quit the team before you've tried out saying maybe.

Be willing to step into a place where your views are different from others. Be willing to entertain other people's ideas. A lot of times we become so rigid about what we believe that we don't make any room for difference. I'm not saying that we need to change our minds every time. If I believe that the earth is round and you say that it's square, I'm probably not going to be open to changing my mind, but I might be open to hearing your opinion.

The word *maybe* is helpful in a lot of situations. It helps us learn to connect well with others. Many times, we don't know the truth about whatever is being discussed, or the truth is based on a perception or experience different from ours. If someone says they experienced something you said as hurtful or confusing, sometimes our knee-jerk reaction is to say, "Well, that's not what happened," or, "No, that's incorrect." And although I completely understand, because what they said isn't clear to you, could what they're saying be true? Could that be their experience? Yeah. Can we give that person room to have their interpretation of the experience? Again, you don't have to change your mind, but can you at least be open to that possibility?

Remaining open to how others interpret the world is a great strategy for reducing conflict in relationships and building connection with people on your team. Be open to the possibility that what you're saying might be interpreted differently by the other person or that they might remember things differently than you or that they might even be a different kind of "historian" than you.

Navigating conflict is a place where people who are stepping out of loneliness and isolation into connection often get stuck. It can be difficult enough as it is to open ourselves up to relationships, embrace *maybe*, and take that first step, but then throw a disagreement or a conflict into the mix and opening ourselves up can seem downright impossible. This is often because our loneliness tells us that we are discounted and unworthy, and conflict seems to confirm that. Because let's face it, if we were valuable, we wouldn't have conflict with others, right?

Wrong.

Healthy conflict is the friction that causes growth in ourselves and others. Jesus knew this, and the Bible is full of stories of Jesus approaching people in kind and loving ways while also telling them hard truths that sometimes led to disagreement. In those moments, Jesus leaned into the relationship instead of out, and for some, that willingness to lean in made all the difference. One of the best ways we can navigate conflict or disagreement is to be careful when deciding what conflict to engage in.

I am a terrible historian. I might say, "This is what happened on Tuesday." And Jodi might say, "Hey, we got the receipts from that day, and I think *this* is actually what happened." I know from experience that when I declare that something has to be true, that's when I'm going to get a lot of resistance, because when I think I have to be right, someone else's knee-jerk reaction will be to argue with me. In that moment, connection really breaks down.

I see people get into a lot of conflict because they argue about who's a better historian. One person says, "On January 10, three years ago, you said . . ." And the other person will say, "Absolutely not. I said . . ." And they argue about it. But here's the thing: there's no way to identify who knows the truth. God didn't give us a tape recorder that we can roll back and listen to what actually was said. It would be awesome if we could do that, but unless we're recording every conversation or conflict that we have, we can't. (And no, I don't recommend recording conversations.)

In that situation, rather than declaring that what the other person says is untrue, say, "Maybe you're right." This admission is more than likely to reduce conflict. When you give someone else permission to feel how they feel and grant the possibility that they're right, they'll respond better to you.

Again, you're not saying they're right without a doubt, you're just saying they might be right.

"I'm not sure you're right, but you might be, and there's really no way to tell. And so I'm okay. I hear where you're coming from. What do we need to do next?"

Why escalate a conflict about something you can't prove anyway? Life is complicated enough.

When you have conflict, make sure it's a conflict that is relevant and can be resolved. Productive conflict can get you somewhere.

Stepping out of isolation and loneliness takes work, whether it's finding the right team or learning to stick around and fill out your jersey even when things don't seem to be working out. Connection is so important, and it's deeper than having a few hundred followers on Instagram who like your photos. True connection requires relationship, which includes vulnerability, trust, and authenticity and isn't found in the shallow end of the pool. It doesn't always come naturally, and it's something most of us must learn to do well, but you will get better at it over time, just like my friend did at football.

> Reflect on when you typically feel the most lonely or isolated. What events, feelings, or circumstances frequently lead you there? Do any of the topics discussed in this chapter come up in those situations? What might you do to step out of loneliness and into connection?

Chapter 19

KNOW YOURSELF

One of my favorite nights of the week is Friday night. Not just because of the obvious TGIF nature of it but because of what it means for our family. It usually means homemade-pizza night, where we catch up as a family, recall the week, watch a funny movie, and sometimes have dance parties. It's a pretty good night that usually carries an enthusiasm and energy that aren't always found in the rest of the week. It's a time for putting too many pepperonis on your pizza, playing music a little too loud, and dancing with your seven-year-old.

It was during one of those times that the subject of Canada Goose coats was brought up. I'm not sure who mentioned it, but someone said that for as cold as it was, we should have warmer coats. (It was probably me.) And so in my excitement, I searched online for the coats, and what did I find but a website selling them for 60 percent off! Wowza! What an incredible night. Jodi was dancing with my youngest son, Finn, as I hurriedly added the coats to the cart, entered my credit card information, and clicked "purchase."

Well, Friday night came and went, but our excitement about our new coats didn't. About two weeks later, a box arrived at the door, and I was pumped. Until I took a closer look at the box. Now, these are supposed to be expensive coats, and so I expected a beautiful box with some tissue paper in it and maybe even one of those fancy envelopes with the receipt. This was a little different. The box was stamped "Origin: China" and it looked like it had been through a lot. There was a rip on the side with some plastic sticking out that I could only assume was our new coats. I was a little concerned.

As I opened the box, I noticed a peculiar smell—not the worst smell but a chemical smell like you'd find in a factory. I pulled my coat out of the bag and found one that looked a lot different from the one I had ordered. I might have been able to live with it if the arm patch on every one of those coats hadn't said "Canada Gose."

I think I laughed at first, but then reality hit me. In my excitement, I had quickly purchased coats without really looking at what they were and where they were from and had unknowingly bought counterfeits. I admit they seemed like pretty good quality coats, other than the patch. They fit well, were in fact warm, and even had fur trim. (Let's not get into what the fur might have been.) But still, they were counterfeits being advertised as something they weren't. We contacted Canada Goose as well as our credit card company and everything was resolved.

You might think this is a story about unknowingly buying a counterfeit coat in the midst of a dance party, but the thing I can't forget is that patch. It reminds me of so many times that I've been perfectly okay just as I am but felt compelled to wear a patch—to say or do something so that someone else would like me. Sometimes we think it's easier to pretend to be someone else. And while that might seem to make so much sense, it takes away from the beauty of who we really are.

I am reminded of a good friend of mine, Daniel, who spent the first two decades of his life attempting to be exactly who his parents and family wanted him to be. He attended all the right schools, got good grades, said and believed the things he should say and believe, and eventually became an attorney. It was tough at times, but Daniel really wanted to do the right thing and be the person that he thought his parents wanted him to be. Maybe you can relate?

The problem was that Daniel wasn't born to be an attorney. He was born to be a botanist who is a Christian and spends his days outside, and it took Daniel a long time to be okay with that. So long that it wasn't until he had created an entire life that was the wrong fit for him that he was able to admit that he had sewn a patch onto his life that wasn't the real thing. Even though Daniel was and is awesome, he felt like he wasn't enough, and so he did his best to be someone else. And, like the Canada "Gose" coat, he did a pretty good job. But he always knew the truth, and it was never far from his mind.

When he could take it no more and finally ripped off the patch, he immediately felt better, but the process of becoming who he actually was became costly. There were conversations to be had and dreams to be pursued, and none of it came easily. But although it took a tremendous amount of work, Daniel always reassured me that ripping off the patch was still easier than wearing it. Sure, he had less money and had to deal with the fallout with his family (who loved him anyway and had only ever wanted for him to be happy), but he didn't have to fake it anymore.

Of all the people I know who have ripped off their patches, I don't know a single one who regretted it. Many would say that it wasn't easy and that it took some work, but many also would say that they were surprised by how many people either already knew their patches weren't authentic or just kept loving them anyway. I often wonder what God thinks when he sees us pretending. Does he feel disappointed, frustrated, sad? I can't pretend to know what God thinks, but I wonder whether he wishes we loved ourselves the way he loves us and that we saw ourselves in the same light he does.

When people come in to my office and start talking about all the things they "should" be better at or "should" have done, I have a kind of snarky response for them: "Stop 'shoulding' on my floor." My response is kind of ridiculous, but so is living the way you or someone else thinks you should. Although there might be lots of reasons to do it, "shoulding" leads only to distraction and hurt when we finally admit to ourselves and others that we are someone else.

Getting rid of this unhealthy self-concept and stepping into who we actually are is also helpful for overcoming what is commonly known as chameleon syndrome, which is a fancy way of saying that you are pretending to be someone you're not. We all tend to don personas to appear to be smarter or more likable, but the happiest people have learned to drop the act and be themselves, no patches required. And when we finally stop covering for ourselves, not only do we often find we're still likable and accepted but also we can start doing better at liking and accepting others.

Where a lot of us pick up the habit of pretending to be someone else is during childhood, and it's often a response to an experience, message, or perception about who we are in relationship to the world. When we are kids, especially, we are all about fitting in: fitting in with our families, our friends, and our classmates. We feel there is little room for us to step very far outside of the norm. Instead, we do our best to be who we imagine we are supposed to be so that we can fit in, get good grades, make people happy, and move on. This works when we have parents and a system that are healthy and encouraging, but it becomes challenging when we don't, because we can end up becoming a person who thrives in an environment that ends after childhood. When as adults we face the prospect of a new life or a different opportunity, we struggle to move toward health because we aren't prepared for it.

Imagine you spent the first eighteen years of your life preparing to be a scuba diver and doing everything you could to fit in with your scuba-diver family, but then when you are eighteen you move to the desert, where there is no water to scuba dive in. Would you stay there, or would you go back to what you knew even if you didn't like it that much? Most of us would go back and avoid the pain of admitting that though we never liked scuba diving, we also didn't like the challenges of learning to live in the desert. And while I can understand this and can even relate to it, this is what happens when we don't live as ourselves. We create a life that isn't ours and raise kids in the same system. It becomes easy to forget why we do what we do and who wanted it anyway.

Maybe as you are reading this chapter, someone in your life comes to mind. Maybe that someone is you. Either way, the question is, "What can I do if I find myself here? How can I break out of what I 'should' be to find who I really am?" Often the answer starts by asking who you are not. I tell you this because I have found, after working with lots of clients and even in my own life, that when we own who we are, it is challenging to identify what we like, want, or think. So it's easier usually to ask, "In what areas am I wearing a counterfeit patch?" Maybe it's a job that you don't like, a shirt that doesn't fit, or a relationship based on an inauthentic version of yourself. My guess is that you know what it is without giving it too much thought. We usually do.

THREE SIGNS
of Chameleon Syndrome

1. Looking to others for your sense of self.
2. Becoming like those around you.
3. Feeling unseen and unheard.

The next step is to take a small step instead of a big one. Although the temptation is usually to begin cutting up and changing big parts of our lives, doing so can be really destructive and cause us more difficulties. Instead, the goal is to take just one step toward authenticity. Taking a big step too quickly is what gets people off track.

I have a question for you: How do you want to be remembered when you die?

I doubt many people have asked you that before. We ask people who they want to be when they grow up, who they want to be in a year, or what's in their five-year plan. But when's the last time you thought about how you want to be remembered? What do you want your legacy to be?

Believe it or not, you're creating a legacy today. You're creating how you'll be viewed forever.

So how would you want to be described?

Let's imagine that later today you will walk outside and get hit by a bus. I hope that doesn't happen. I want you to be healthy and happy for a long time, but let's say that does happen to you. Guess what? Your legacy starts now. And it's probably not how and when you thought your legacy would begin, but we have no guarantee how long we will be on this earth. So we must consider that our forever could start at any time.

Your legacy is more important than any other plan you're going to make in your life. When we make one-year plans or five-year plans, it all sounds great, but nothing is guaranteed. What's guaranteed is today. This minute. This moment. And not much beyond that. And I'm sorry about that, because for me, that's sometimes a difficult pill to swallow.

So who do you want to be when you die? How close are you to being that person today? If the person you are today is pretty different from the person you want to be when you die, then how do you become that person? Because you can start today.

If you want to be remembered as a kind person, be kind to people today. If you want to be remembered for being generous, be generous today.

Now, you might have some huge goals. You might want to be a guy whose legacy is being out of debt, but you have $20,000 in credit card debt. So you could pay $20 on your debt today, and that step gets you closer to your goal.

If you want your legacy to be that you were a loving husband, but you're currently yelling at your wife, today's as good a time as any to change your legacy.

We started building our legacy the day we were born, and if we don't like how it looks, it's up to us to do something about it.

We'd all love to have an amazing legacy, that highlights our successes and skips over our failures. We want to be remembered only for the good things we did and none of the bad. That's definitely what I want. But it might not be what I get, and that's reality. So that means if I check out today, I'll be remembered for who I am today. Not anything else. I won't be remembered as the guy I could have been five years from now. And when you get down to it, the trappings and titles and all those things that seem so important don't matter as much. They're actually what follow a life well lived. It's character that counts.

When we know who we want to be when we die, it becomes easier to be that person right now. It doesn't mean you won't ever make a mistake. But being that person can and does get easier. And when we do that work, when we aim to become that person, connection with others is easier because we know ourselves.

Thinking this way led me to realize I needed both practical knowledge (part 1 of this book) and action (part 2) to deal with my grief over the hurts I'd experienced, the things I'd lost, and the opportunities I'd ruined so I could find connection again. At some point it made sense to me that we need to integrate the head and the heart to bring our feelings to light and deal with them together. The idea is to "lean in" and commit to feeling our feelings by acknowledging them, talking about them, and processing them, which drives us to connection.

This is how we learn to become new people who love well. We bring together pain and love and live them both: the facts of love and the actions of the heart together. Emotional connection requires emotion *and* taking action to reach out. By doing both, you can build a new identity, own it, and be changed. We have been studying the principles that help us understand the heart, but we also need to practice applying them. This new you will become more attuned to the work involved in creating the legacy you want to leave. It's not about doing everything right. It's about being vulnerable and willing to try and fail if need be before getting it right.

Take a couple of minutes to write down the character traits you want to be known for. Maybe they are bravery, resilience, or persistence. How do those character traits show up in your life today? How might you behave differently if they are important to you?

PART 3

------->

EMBRACING
YOUR CONNECTION

By now you have come to understand that getting past your past is more than something you say and instead is something that you do often. It's not just a sentiment but a lifestyle, and embracing it requires more than facing problems or learning about love. It also requires connection.

Connection is the part of the process of healing that is often overlooked, because it's one thing to heal from an injury and another thing entirely to get back onto the field. Getting back onto the field is scary. It requires risk and uncertainty. But if we don't embrace connection, we can become filled with regret because deep down we know that we stopped short of the life we could have and should have lived.

I want to help you avoid that, by building a community and solidifying your new mindset, but it will require you to take one last step. You'll have to get back out there again.

Chapter 20

BE YOURSELF

Several years ago I was invited to go skiing and snowboarding with my in-laws over Christmas. I'd never been skiing or snowboarding and thought the trip was a great idea. I mean, I'd done some rollerblading (remember how well that went?!), how difficult could skiing and snowboarding be? But more important than the activity itself was that Jodi's brothers, who were seasoned snowboarders, really wanted me to go with them, and I'd always wanted them to like me. So I rented a snowboard and helmet and headed to the ski shack at the bottom of the hill.

I think it was probably when I couldn't get my board strapped to my feet that I got nervous. I was definitely on-edge by the time I jumped haphazardly onto the ski lift that took me and my brothers-in-law up to the regular ski hill. As we joked on the way up, I knew I was making a mistake. How much of a mistake was foreshadowed when I got stuck trying to get off the lift and was dragged around a bit. Things were getting ugly already.

And yet this series of unfortunate events didn't stop me from wanting to snowboard down the mountain that day. I love Jodi's brothers, and looking back, I so desperately wanted to be part of the group. As everyone took off on their boards, I lagged behind at the top of the hill before pushing off and picking up speed. For a moment, I felt pretty good about myself. Maybe I was the one guy in the world who had never snowboarded before but would somehow pick it up his first time down the mountain. But then it hit me like, well, a twenty-foot-tall spruce tree, which brought my grand snowboarding adventure to a sudden and painful halt.

I rolled over, glad to be alive after my collision with the tree, but my face felt like it had been punched by someone holding a handful of tacks. Not that long after my crash, the ski patrol came to my rescue. Because I was bleeding pretty badly from my face, they decided to pull me back to the ski shack on the medical sled. By this time Jodi's brothers had long since finished their run and were (thankfully) nowhere in sight.

I had been on the sled for only a minute when my phone rang. I fought through the twenty layers of clothing I was wearing to get to the phone, carefully trying not to flip the sled, and answered. One of my brothers-in-law said they had missed me on the hill and asked where I was. My reply was cut short when I looked over to see the rest of the guys heading down the hill now watching me being pulled along on the medical sled in all my injured glory. But rather than making fun of me, my brother-in-law asked if I was okay.

"I've actually never snowboarded before," I told him.

"Then why did you want to start by snowboarding down a big hill rather than on the bunny hill?!" he asked.

I told him I thought I could handle the bigger hill. But I knew better. I had pretended I knew what I was doing because I hadn't wanted to be left out. I wanted to fit in with the group even if it meant attempting something I'd never done before. Weirdly enough, my brothers-in-law stayed with me for a while in the bunny area after I was cleared to leave the medical shack. They didn't care whether I knew what I was doing. They just wanted to hang out with me, even if it meant we had to snowboard down the bunny hill.

Sometimes we think of God and others the way I thought of my brothers-in-law that day. We so badly want connection that we'll risk injury by faking it just to get that connection we desire. What's refreshing (and disappointing) about faking it, though, is that we'll often crash many times along the way when we didn't really need to in the first place.

If I had just been myself that day, I wouldn't have crashed. And I might have had more fun. Actually, I *know* I would have had a *lot* more fun, since I wouldn't have crashed into a tree.

I don't know about you, but there have been so many times when I could just feel in my gut that what I was doing was missing the mark of what I actually needed. I wonder sometimes what would have happened if I had listened to God before going down that hill or doing something else that I shouldn't have done. If I had just been myself in the first place, would I have been accepted? Would God still love me even if I didn't pray fifty times a day or have the consistency in my relationship with him that I think I should? Or is it better to fake it and ignore that gut feeling when it comes to showing my true self to God and others?

Clearly, in the snowboarding situation, it would have been better to be myself. But I think that's true of a lot of situations.

It saves us time when we decide to be ourselves from the beginning, allowing people to accept us or not for who we are right off the bat, instead of deciding later we're not a good fit because we were just faking it to be accepted.

This reminds me of the story of Watson Thornton, a missionary in Japan who wanted to join the Japan Evangelistic Band. Watson decided to pay a visit to the group's leader, who lived several hours away. Just before boarding the train to go see the guy, Watson felt something in his gut telling him to wait. Four more opportunities to get on the train came and went, and Watson eventually missed the last train, believing he must not have been meant to travel that day. As he began to leave the train station to return home, Watson heard someone yell his name, and he turned to see the leader he was hoping to meet standing there at the station.*

I think about how difficult it would be to watch train after train depart the station and choose to listen to my gut instead. On a good day I could probably miss two trains. But four? That's doubtful. And yet God calls us to do just that sometimes. I find this truth both beautiful and frustrating, but God does not always use a giant LED screen at the airport to give us instructions. Sometimes it's a feeling in our gut that we just can't shake that points us in the right direction.

Just like it did for Watson. Just like it would have for me on the slopes that day, had I listened.

That gut feeling is, often, telling us something that's not necessarily easy, something we maybe don't want to hear.

---

* John Koessler, *Practicing the Present: The Neglected Art of Living in the Now* (Chicago: Moody, 2019), 121–22.

For Watson, it was telling him to wait. And for me, my gut feeling—God—was telling me to simply be myself.

Maybe you're reading this and you know that feeling or are experiencing it now. If so, listen to what your gut is telling you. It might require some patience, but chances are it's God pointing you in the right direction.

I know that many times in my life God has pointed me in the right direction by getting me to listen to my gut. It's not usually easy, but things worth doing often aren't.

One example is when I felt called to leave my job to attend college and become a counselor. I was in the best financial spot I had been in for a long time. I had a stable job where I managed two hundred employees and had a weekly revenue of 100k. For once in my life, I felt I was doing well and could be proud of myself. And yet I was feeling called to a new career and would have to go to school for several years, only to make much less than I was making at the time. But our gut doesn't care about weekly revenues, and neither does God.

God doesn't call us to do what's easy. He calls us to our potential.

I can't say that I listened right away or that I never had doubts (I did, pretty often). But I kept at it. And I learned that although we sometimes think that God leaves us when we're confused or hurt or unsure, what's more often the case is that we don't listen. So if we want the life that we are called to, we have to listen to God and to our gut, even when it's uncomfortable or inconvenient.

Even though Watson and I had gut feelings about different things, our gut feelings led to the same outcome: connection. Watson connected with the leader of the evangelistic group, and I connected with a career I love and, later, my brothers-in-law (after a run-in with a tree).

But connection is a lot easier when we listen to that "gentle whisper" of God (1 Kings 19:11–13) inside us right away. His voice doesn't usually give us easy answers or quick fixes, but what it does tell us are truths we've probably known about ourselves all along.

> Today will you choose to trust that voice and be yourself, no matter how you think other people might react? Being yourself, being vulnerable, is scary. But it's a lot less painful than running into a tree because you pretended you knew how to snowboard.

Chapter 21

COURAGE IS REQUIRED

When you're a counselor, you really luck out if you like personal development, because you spend most of your life doing a lot of personal development in the name of being a better counselor. So as part of some personal development work, I was able to do some training at this amazing facility with a few clinicians and staff who are well-known in the field, along with several colleagues I didn't know from around the country.

As part of the training process, I and the other attendees were expected to do the personal development work ourselves. In this way we would know what it's like to go through the exercises and experience the growth that comes with them. One of the training exercises that was the most profound for me included a group experience in which everyone came together to show support for each other and to connect.

Everyone in the room would surround one person and say affirmations over them. I'd never had that kind of thing happen to me before. I've never had so many people in one room come together to say that they loved and cared about me, noticed something about me, or wanted the best for me. And part of the reason why I'd never experienced that is because I'd never let something like that happen before. I was sure that I'd be my typical self and sit in the back of the room where I could check out mentally and leave before everyone else. But for some reason, this time I let people in. It felt terrifying to be connected. I'd been loved well before, but it felt terrifying to accept that level of connection from other people and not dismiss it or fix it, just receive it.

It takes courage to connect.

Many of us don't pursue this level of connection unless we have to. Had I not been at this training session and gone through this exercise where people said kind things about me—which I sweated about for hours before it actually happened—I wouldn't have experienced that connection. But I was in a safe place with people who cared about me, and I took the risk.

That's really what connection is about: the courage to let ourselves be loved. When we find that courage, we also see that there are people around us who are able and willing to love us if we'll let them.

Mike has become one of my best friends, although I never would have expected it. We started working at Bethesda Workshops in Nashville, and I met him when we did some intensive workshops together to help individuals and couples struggling with and affected by sexual addiction. For the workshops, we had to travel and stay at hotels, and I had to share a room with Mike, which I dreaded. When you're a kid, sharing a hotel room with your friends or family is this grand adventure, but as an adult, it's never as fun to share a room. Adults just want to sleep as much as we can and not be bothered, but there's a sort of beauty to being forced to share space and have community like that (even if you probably won't get as much sleep as you want to).

So Mike, this person who, again, I would have just as well preferred not to have a connection with (and have my own hotel room away from), was a guy I ended up spending a lot of time with. One night before a workshop, we were in our room and I was ironing my dress shirt, trying to mind my own introverted business and be as private as possible. But I could not get the ironing board to close.

There I stood in my pajamas, having just finished ironing my shirt (and done a beautiful job, I might add), unable to get the ironing board shut. I started wrestling it, which I'm sure was hilarious for Mike to watch from his side of the room, when eventually Mike stood up and asked, "Hey, why don't I help you with that?"

We wrestled with the thing together—two grown men attempting to collapse an ironing board.

Now, before you judge us too harshly, the ironing boards in hotels are typically pretty tough to fold. But there we were, two guys at eleven o'clock at night, trying to get an ironing board closed, both preferring to mind our own business, yet committed to solving this problem. We were about ten minutes into attempting to get the best of the board when we realized how ridiculous we must look. We never did get it folded up. We ended up leaving it out. But we were laughing the whole time, and that connection between us remains today.

Mike and I are still great friends. We don't fold ironing

boards up together very often or share hotel rooms anymore, but the point is that sometimes you have to be vulnerable enough to let someone help you and wrestle a problem together. Of course, that level of vulnerability feels awkward, especially when you're in your PJs in a hotel room with someone you don't know very well. This is where courage comes in. We have to courageously fold an ironing board up with someone to make a connection. Beautiful things will come from courage, if you let it.

Sometimes God puts ironing boards in our lives as opportunities to connect with others. Sometimes God gives us situations where we have to be vulnerable and real to connect in an authentic way. We only have to embrace these situations with courage and a willingness to look dumb in front of someone we don't know very well.

But the opposite can also be true. Sure, connections are made through big moments of vulnerability at a workshop where you don't know anyone, but I think sometimes we believe we can leverage some false courage, take a big leap, and show others our true colors all in one well-choreographed motion without having to do the hard work of being there, day in and day out.

Though courage is required for connection, sometimes one moment of dumb courage can paint a false picture of a person. At least that's what I learned from an unfortunately placed snake in a river.

When I was in my teens, the popular place to go was the state park. It had a pretty high bridge connecting two large rock faces. Rumor had it that at one time a bank robber jumped between the cliffs on a horse, which seems a little tough to believe now that I'm not a teenage boy, but we would hang out at the bridge whenever the cool kids had parties. I typically wasn't invited to the parties, but on one occasion I was invited to hang at the bridge with some friends and a group of girls. We wanted to impress the girls, and the most impressive thing we could come up with was to jump off the bridge into the water below.

Now, we had no idea how deep the river was. But one boy was braver than the rest of us and decided to jump.

He stripped down to his shorts, looking back at the girls, who were staring at him with glee. Then he jumped! It was glorious, really. I mean, I was terrified for him, but he jumped feet first into the water. Much to our shame, he seemed fine. He hadn't drowned. But as he was swimming to shore, we all saw something in the water about two feet away from where he had gone in.

It was a giant water moccasin, and it was swimming toward him.

I don't know whether snakes really swim, but this snake was, let's say, edging closer and closer, seemingly directly at the kid.

Now this brave young man who had just impressed so many women, who was, I was sure, about to be filling his calendar with dates, suddenly began screaming and screaming. As the snake got closer and closer, his screams got louder and higher. I guess the snake decided this kid wasn't worth the trouble, because it swam away, but the effect of the boy's courageous jump was quickly erased by his screaming.

What still stands out to me about this incident is that I would have been more afraid of the water and the fall than of the snake in the river, but the water and the fall didn't scare the boy at all. He took that risk. But the snake scared him to death—which, hey, I'm right there with you, pal—and that lost him the admiration he had earned with the girls for jumping in the first place.

He risked his life for nothing because we remembered him as the guy who screamed because he was afraid of a snake, not as the guy who jumped off a bridge because he was so brave.

I think about the number of times I've tried to do something that wasn't good for me in an effort to win someone over or earn their respect, but because I hadn't fully considered the risk, what I did was more dangerous or less fulfilling than I'd anticipated.

We all have bridges in our lives from which we look down and think jumping is going to make all the difference. *When I jump off this bridge into the water below, things are going to change for me. People are going to respect me. People are going to think I'm different.* But that's not usually what happens. I wish it were, but usually a cataclysmic moment only changes things negatively. The things we really long for, like respect, perspective, community, and relationships, instead are earned through many small courageous experiences of being authentic, a far greater currency than any bridge you could jump off.

The courage required for connection is not often the courage we think of. The kid who jumped off the bridge had courage, sure. But it wasn't authentic, as we all saw when he screamed at the snake. His courage came from a desire to impress the girls who were watching that day. When we want real connection, not just a pat on the back or for people to think we're cool, we need courage that risks something personal.

- The courage to look dumb in front of someone you don't know super well.
- The courage to ask a question you are hesitant to ask.
- The courage to step out on a limb and risk being rejected.
- The courage to be fully known for who you are, flaws and all.
- The courage to be truly loved.

Such courage desires authentic connection above all.

When I think back on the bridge story, I remember the laughter we shared when we knew for sure our friend was okay and as we recollected the way he screamed and flailed his arms when he saw the snake, which it turned out hadn't been after him at all. The real lesson learned that day was that no matter how hard you try to impress people, if you're not authentic and don't consider the risk, you only end up soaking wet and screaming.

Let me tell you about DJ JVR. Sometime in my twenties, someone told me that because I liked electronic music, which was pretty popular at the time, I should become a DJ. Now, I will tell you, and Jodi will tell you, and other people will tell you, that I don't have a lot of rhythm. So obviously I was going to be a great hit. I remember that as I was ordering the turntable, records, and headphones (on the credit card that I couldn't pay off), I felt I was taking a leap into the unknown.

I think it was when I opened the box and didn't know how

to use the record player that I wondered whether this was a bad idea. But I had already told everyone that I was a DJ, so it didn't really matter. When I showed up at a house party for my first gig, I realized I had made a terrible mistake. The actual DJ was DJ-ing and people were dancing and having a good time as I made my way to the booth, nervous and sweaty, unsure even of where I was supposed to stand. But I told myself none of that mattered because this was my time to shine. This was my jump. So as the real DJ introduced me over the roar of the party and the music thumping loudly, I told myself all I had to do was make it through the next thirty minutes.

Somewhere in my mind I thought it would be a great idea to yell, "Drop the beat!" In my head I imagined the party erupting into cheers and the police coming because everyone was having so much fun. What I did not imagine was yelling "drop the beat" way too close to the microphone and at a point when the song was ending, not dropping. When I screamed, "Drop the beat!" and looked out and saw a sea of confused faces, I knew the jig was up.

My DJ career ended there. I'm not even sure I brought my equipment home. But I realized that a jump makes sense only if God is cheering you on. If he's not, it often will end badly.

An example of this is in the months leading up to our engagement. I knew Jodi was the one. I also knew that getting engaged meant taking a jump. For me, it was such a loaded moment. I hadn't seen many marriages work, I had a lot of baggage, and I wasn't sure who I was. But I knew God was telling me to jump—that it was for the right reasons and that it would be okay. When I mustered up the courage to propose, it was not at a fancy restaurant or a packed house party. I did not look cool or rich or accomplished. I knelt on the floor in my efficiency apartment where Jodi sat on the futon I'd barely had money to purchase. I knew that it was a jump I couldn't take back and that if she said no, it would hurt. I also knew that God was there cheering me on. And so I jumped. I learned that sometimes we have to jump even when we can't see the other side. That kind of jump is possible if God is in on the deal.

My challenge for you today is to think about the decisions you're making. Are you making them for yourself, or for someone else? If you were being yourself and showing up in an authentic way, how would your life look different?

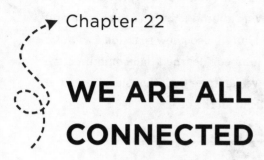

Chapter 22

WE ARE ALL CONNECTED

My daughter loves unicorns. She loves them so much that one of the many unicorn-related items on her birthday list was unicorn poop. My daughter will tell you that unicorns are her favorite because they're magical and, above all else, special. And she's right. I mean, no one is buying a toy called raccoon poop.

But I tell you this to assure you that though you are special too, you aren't a unicorn. Although you might think you're unique, I would gently suggest that you are more like others than you are different from them. Whether you make a gazillion dollars, are a pro athlete, work at a magical chocolate factory, or something else, you probably still have a lot in common with everyone else.

And that's sort of fantastic news.

Because when we tell ourselves that our experience of life is so much different from others' or that we can't relate to anyone, it separates us from people and stands in the way of connection.

One of my favorite verses in the Bible (Eccl. 1:9) talks about how there is nothing new under the sun, and I think that applies here. To get better, to work through any external or internal obstacle, you'll have to do the same things the person you think is beneath you has to do. We have to understand that we all have problems, and that our problems aren't really that much different from others'.

This similarity is something I learned both personally and as a therapist. When I began my career, I worked a great deal with persons who were either going to prison or getting out of prison. It was both challenging and rewarding work, and I feel honored to have had those experiences. I spent lots of time helping clients with vulnerability, emotional regulation, relationship skills, and coping. And for a while, I believed that the work I was doing with them was very different from what I was doing with anyone else.

As I advanced in my career, I spent less time working with that population and more with executive-level clients and couples. My assumption was that I'd be working on a completely different set of problems with this new group of people, and I was surprised to learn the problems were actually similar. I was still talking about all of the same core concepts, just using different language. Instead of apartments, Toyotas, and hourly wages, I now spoke to people about owning apartment complexes, Ferraris, and salaries. Although the brands and sizes changed, the key elements were the same. Some days, I would have a wealthy or successful client followed by an ex-convict and find myself having a very similar conversation in both sessions.

It's comforting to know that we all share the basics. We all have the same emotions, we all struggle with relationships and with working toward goals, and we all have pain. Because of this, we are connected, and it's in that connection that we find healing.

I think Jesus really captured this concept in his life. He would approach anyone to talk with them. He never said, "Well, that person is too special," or, "That person is too messed up." Instead, each was simply a person he might connect with and help. Jesus helped tax collectors, lepers, and prostitutes as well as officials and followers. Jesus just sees all of us as people.

This is an important concept for two reasons: sometimes we think we are too bad off to ask for help, and other times we think we are not bad off enough.

Maybe it's difficult to ask for help because you feel you are:

- Too broken
- Too successful
- Too far gone
- The only one
- Responsible to solve it on your own

Can you relate to any of these?

So many of us can at one time or another. But the reality is that these are lies we tell ourselves that get in the way of our asking for help or giving help to others. Imagine that Jesus believed any of these statements. The Bible would be a much different and shorter book. Instead, there are many stories in the Bible that tell us that we are all worthy of saving and of love regardless of who we are or what we have done.

You might be thinking, "But Jason, you don't understand. I struggle with [blank]. No one else can relate or help me."

I get it and am sorry to hear it, but you aren't the only one. It may feel that you are because someone may have told you that or the shame you felt communicated it to you, but it's simply not true. What's true is that whatever is keeping you awake at night or compels you to change the subject when it comes up in conversation is rooted in a shame that tells you you are alone.

Shame says that you are too far broken, messed up, different to ask for help or connect with others, but Jesus says he loves you just the same.

We all have things to learn. We all must remain curious and be courageous. If we do things right and acknowledge that we all must do the same internal work, we might find that we can connect with others better than we ever thought possible.

We're all a lot more connected than we've come to believe, for bad and for good.

You are also not worse than anyone else. I know this might tick some people off, but you know the person on the news who got busted for driving while intoxicated? Or your buddy who was fired from his job for poor performance? You and I have a lot in common with those guys. We've just gotten luckier, been given more grace, or had more tools to avoid such outcomes. Being similar to these people might seem like a bad thing, but it's all about perspective. From my vantage point, realizing that we all have similar capacities to make wise or poor choices allows us to truly be seen by others, where before we might have felt like we had to hide.

We all have stuff in our lives that's good and stuff that's bad. We're all on the same playing field.

Protect that sameness and return to it when you are hurting and feel alone. Some individuals' experiences have included abuse of one kind or another, leaving them wounded. I can relate, and for a long time I walked around with wounds that really should have been treated rather than covered up. Coming out of childhood, I had lots of feelings, experiences, and beliefs that should have been brought into the light. But what I told myself instead is that what I had been through was too different from and also not as bad as what others had experienced, and so talking about it would be a waste of other people's time and I should figure it out myself.

This belief cost me several years of my life and many opportunities, including:

- Going to art school for painting
- Finishing college
- Moving to a different city
- Backpacking through Europe
- Getting a dog
- Showing up as a healthy father and husband from the start

These things hurt me far more than my problems ever did. They are the things that if you aren't careful, sneak into your head in the middle of the night and cause you to lie there for a while. They hurt. And all are because I was "too this" or "not enough that" to talk to someone and get the help I needed. For years I believed that I couldn't, and that belief cost me. What I know now is that my path is my path, and that while there will be things I think I've missed out on, it's not my plan that I am carrying out, and so I have peace about it. But if I had a time machine, the first thing I'd do is go back to eighteen-year-old

Jason to urge him to talk about the things he thinks can't be spoken about.

If we don't try to get help, the wound never really heals, eventually becoming something we need to medicate. Maybe this is why you continue to return to pornography or alcohol: you are trying to heal this wound. But the truth is, that kind of medication won't work anymore.

When we make that leap and realize our problems aren't so unique, that we're not unicorns, it becomes easier to take the necessary steps to connect with those around us, seek help, and build the community we all so desperately crave.

And when we know we're not unicorns, we don't have to be all that special to know we're worth knowing, and that's plenty special.

Like every other growth goal we set, it requires practice. This is true for all of us, not just some. We're all connected in this lifelong work to become better at loving and receiving love—for ourselves and others. And this connection requires the same things of everyone, most of all taking action.

> Think about a time recently you realized we're all connected or more alike than we are different. Was that a comforting or concerning thing to you? Why do you think you had that response?

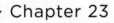

Chapter 23

CONNECTION REQUIRES ACTION

In my twenties and thirties I played squash occasionally with my brother. Together, we'd put on the glasses and gloves and grab our racquets and walk through the tiny door into the court. (Why such a tiny door, I wonder.) From there it would usually get ugly. Overweight, poor coordination, ugly. For those who don't know, a squash ball doesn't bounce much. It's made so that it can't bounce much. This apparently makes the game more challenging and thus more interesting.

What I learned after hours of losing to my brother is that to win in squash you need to always be close to the ball, and when it bounces (no matter how small the bounce), you have to be ready to act. If you aren't close to the ball, it will often take too much time to get to it and you'll miss your opportunity to catch it on the bounce.

I think our lives are like that. We sometimes want huge opportunities (work, finances, relationships) to appear that are obvious to us, but we don't always get that luxury. Instead, sometimes the opportunities are subtle and require us to be close to take action.

This means we need a great deal of focus on what matters in life if we are to realize our full potential. Without that, we will sprint exhaustedly through the court of life swinging wildly all the way.

There have been times in my life when I ran, swinging wildly with my racquet hissing through the air, because I lost focus on what I was being called to do. It stands to reason that some of our most difficult seasons are this way: full of swinging and exhaustion, running from one place to the next.

When you are struggling in squash, you need to stop, stand for a moment, and locate the ball. This is often difficult because it means you have to overcome the urge to run to where the ball is. By the time you get there, it will be gone. However, by stopping you can see where the ball is going, and this makes all the difference.

If you feel like you have been running around and are exhausted, stop. Watch for the ball and go where it's going rather than where it is now. It will make all the difference.

Seizing opportunities in life requires action, but so does connection. Actually, connection is an opportunity we don't always take the proper action to embrace. Just like we can't sit there and wait for the ball to come to us in squash, we can't wait for connection to come to us. Connection requires action.

There is a show on television called *Who Wants to Be a Millionaire?* where contestants are asked a series of questions, each more difficult than the one before. If contestants are able to answer each question correctly, they win one million dollars. Pretty sweet, right?

Along the way, if you get stuck, you have some options to ask for help, one of which is to call someone you know. Sounds simple enough, but what do you do when your friend doesn't answer?

On an episode in January 2019, a contestant phoned a friend, who missed the call the first time. Luckily he answered the second go around, but can you imagine? The pressure of sitting there needing someone to pick up and hearing it go to voicemail?

I'd say that there is more at stake on this show than the million dollars it offers. What's at stake is connection with others, fulfillment, meaning, and purpose, and those are hard to put a pricetag on.

I know what you're thinking: "Jason, no one answers their phone or makes calls anymore." I agree. We don't. But I'm not here to argue that it's a good thing. We have gotten more and more okay with the fact that we don't connect anymore. This has led us to feel increasingly isolated and alone despite carrying around in our pockets a device that can connect us all day long.

I know it has been said a million times before, but we have to be the friend we want to have, and sometimes that means making the first move. We have to initiate. We have to take that first step. Send the text message. Make the call. Invite that person to coffee. Start the recurring dinner plan.

It's not easy, and lots of times it's awkward, but you're not going to get any closer to the connection you desire just by sitting there waiting for it to come to you.

A manager of mine once gave me the book *You Can't Teach a Kid to Ride a Bike at a Seminar*. In addition to having a great title, the book is pretty brilliant and makes an obvious point.*

The point of the book is that sometimes we spend a significant amount of time reading or learning about how to do something rather than just doing it. This is because learning about it always feels safer, lulling us into a sense of stuckness and complacency. Mostly because of the internet and social media, it really isn't possible to know everything before you try something. There is just too much information out there. But if we aren't careful, it can be easy to get stuck in research mode.

Are you in research mode when it comes to connection right now:

- Spending all of your time dreaming up ideal scenarios of what your community should look like but never actually doing anything about it?
- Getting resentful toward that friend who never visits for the weekend but not making plans for a trip yourself?
- Wishing you called each other more without actually picking up the phone?

My twenties and thirties were my research-mode years. Sure, I did some things, but I also did much more studying than doing. It just felt safer. But this also led to constantly feeling like I wasn't doing enough and couldn't do enough to be successful.

---

* David H. Sandler and John Hayes, *You Can't Teach a Kid to Ride a Bike at a Seminar* (New York: Dutton, 1995).

Eventually I had to get on the bike and ride, which is sometimes easier said than done.

When I was a kid, I turned my bicycle upside down on the sidewalk to learn more before riding it, spinning the tire faster and faster until eventually my chubby finger got in the way of the spokes and the wheel ate it like a starving finger-eating beast, and it broke my finger. I think of this moment often. I have the slightest scar on my finger from this incident, and it reinforces the point I'm trying to make.

Sometimes we don't need to learn more. We just need to ride the bike. Because if we don't, there can be pain in that too. There really is no way to avoid pain. But chances are that if we ride the bike, at least we get to see something new and feel something we haven't felt before.

Sure, it might be awkward to make that call to a friend you haven't seen in a while or to ask to go to lunch with a coworker you want to get to know better, but what's the alternative? People can hurt you, annoy you, betray you, or stop being your friend for no real reason, but isn't it better to have tried for connection than never to have tried at all?

Think of how Jesus simply walked around and asked the disciples to follow him. Each time I read those passages in the Bible, I'm shocked that the disciples just went along with Jesus and didn't ask to have a couple of months to consider his proposition or look over the projected numbers first. (I think I would have.) They just went along with Jesus into their new lives. Were there injuries along the way? Absolutely. But there were also beautiful experiences and a larger purpose to be found.

The same is true of you and me. As we seek deeper connection with those around us, we might get hit in the face with the ball from time to time or miss it entirely, but there is also so much to be gained.

We need to take action.

> One of my favorite verses is Isaiah 6:8, where Isaiah says, "Here am I. Send me!" Have you been feeling called to a task, a place, a conversation, or an action? Chances are you know what it is. What is one small step that you can take toward that goal today?

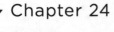

Chapter 24

CONNECTION REQUIRES COMMUNICATION

No matter how you look at it, connection will not happen without some type of communication. Even if the connection is nonverbal, we need it to connect with others. What's challenging is that at times communication can require some vulnerability. This idea is defined through the concept of communication silos.

Where I'm from in the Midwest, we have a lot of silos. If you're fortunate enough to live in warmer climes, you probably know that a silo, or a grain bin, is a metal structure that holds corn or soybeans. It's basically this giant light-colored houselike thing—a vertical column that maybe has several other vertical columns next to it, but the columns aren't connected in any way. The idea is that if departments within an organization don't communicate, they can become like silos, operating on their own, never asking another department for help or feedback.

Accounting might not talk to HR, or vice versa. Maybe HR

is saying we need to hire someone. Well, accounting says we don't have the money for that, but accounting doesn't have a conversation with HR because they're not connected; they're separate silos. No conversation happens until after HR hires the person and accounting complains.

Relational silos in a business are, as you can see, not exactly a great thing. Often this communication style costs a business potential clients. It costs money. And it affects the community and morale of the office.

We can extend this idea of relational silos into our personal relationships and marriages. Now more than ever, we're so isolated that we're in danger of becoming silos that simply exist next to one another. We don't connect. We have lots of information about the other person in the relationship, but we use it just to serve ourselves.

This can play out in a lot of ways. One way we see it happening is in the sharing of information. Imagine your partner selling one of your cars or repainting the bathroom without talking to you first. You would like to have been consulted. Or imagine your partner neglecting to tell you about a major bill. You would feel surprised and maybe upset when it comes due. When this lack of communication is at its worst, relationships can actually end because people feel so alone and without incentive to be in the relationship any longer. The difficult thing is that our current lifestyle and culture encourage us to operate in a silo-like fashion. We're consuming things, we're storing things, and we don't always need to share those things with the people we love or care about. We might share surface-level things, but we're not really sharing what we need to.

Instead, we need to be sharing things that are important

with our partner—things that relate to our relationship or our life that they would need to know, plus things that are important to us, including our feelings and needs.

So how do we get out of a cycle of relational isolation? One way is by holding a weekly meeting with your spouse where you connect on issues, or you build a bridge between your silos with things that are relevant and important to you. Begin these weekly meetings by showing up authentically.

Showing up in an authentic way means being honest and talking about feelings. I know it's a real therapist thing to say, but we need to talk about feelings and needs and desires intentionally. Power comes into the room when we've planned to have a conversation to ask for what we need and to talk about what's going on with us. I would challenge you to practice this type of communication often. Acknowledge when you feel you're in a relational silo or when you feel others have siloed away from you, and share why. It's always possible to bridge the gap between silos. But if we're not careful, our silos will grow farther and farther apart because we haven't dealt with our feelings.

It gets worse the longer this goes on, right? Silos are made of steel. And if they become reinforced with metal, it's even more difficult to get through and make a connection with another person.

When we think about silos, the good stuff—the grain and corn—is on the inside, right? So let's talk about people this same way. The good stuff is on the inside—your heart, feelings, wants, desires. If we are silent for too long, those feelings act up.

They become less accessible, and connection is difficult. Maybe you grew up in a household of relational silos, where Mom and Dad seemed to just exist on their own and you had little to no connection with them. The idea of opening up to reveal your good stuff might be difficult for you to grasp because you were never shown how to communicate in a healthy way.

As you practice opening up to your spouse or in your other relationships, realize that the first couple of times you talk or have that meeting, it's going to seem awkward and uncomfortable. It's going to seem a whole lot easier not to do it. And guess what? You're right. It is easier to continue to live in a silo than it is to open up to another person. But the truth is, it will not get easier unless you practice. This can be a bit challenging because you have to simply try and see what happens.

I have often approached a conversation, especially a challenging one, with the idea that somehow I could come up with exactly the right thing to say. I'd agonize over each and every word, thinking about whether it might not be perfect. This is not practicing communication. This is stewing in anxiety. After looking for just the right phrase for a while, I often realize that there is no perfect thing to say. Sometimes practicing communication means we just need to say *something*.

A good friend of mine named Tim passed away at a young age from cancer. It was an aggressive form of cancer, and within a year, this person I had known as high-functioning and independent became bed ridden and was struggling to care for himself. It was a sad and difficult thing to watch.

Toward the end, I received a call from Tim's wife, who said it was time to visit him one last time. I had gotten calls like this before, but I struggled with this one because of how close we had been and how quickly everything had happened. I also had almost no time to prepare the perfect thing to say to someone so important to me on the last time I saw him.

As I drove to the hospice-care center, the sun pierced my car windows and I felt the warmth on my face and started to cry. I didn't know what to say to Tim. As a therapist, I should have had something great to share. Maybe a quote or song lyrics or something better than what I could come up with on my own. But I didn't have any of those things. I was just sad to be losing my friend.

I pulled up to the hospice center and got out of my car feeling like a kid who hadn't studied for his semester tests, and walked sheepishly into my friend's room feeling like the biggest fraud ever. As I spoke to Tim's wife and sat by his bedside, my anxiety soared. Rather than saying anything, tears simply ran down my face. I was sure I had let my friend down by not having anything profound to say.

Under a tremendous burden of guilt, I looked at Tim and said, "I know that I'm supposed to say something amazing right now, but I have nothing. I want you to know that this is so important to me to show you that I care, but I just couldn't get it right."

When people know your heart, they know your heart. They don't need to hear you say something specific, they just need to hear you. Tim looked at me, smiled, and said, "Jason, I just needed you to come here, sit down, and say anything."

Tim went on to tell me that throughout his illness, he kept trying to do and say all the right things to his wife and kids but learned early on that trying to say the perfect thing resulted only in having less time. Tim said he realized that what was the most important to those around him was just saying something, anything at all.

I nodded and smiled. Tim had always been a step ahead of me and it made sense that even in this moment when I felt like I should give him something, instead he gave me something. We talked for a while and said our goodbyes. Tim passed away the next day, but what he said to me that day forever affected my life in a major way.

Communication doesn't have to be perfect to foster connection, it just has to be there.

Is there something you need to say to someone that you have been overthinking? Maybe it's time to say what's true even if it's not perfect. If the person knows your heart, they won't mind, and you just might have more connection as a result.

EPILOGUE

It had been a hot couple of weeks. Our whole family was still recovering from getting sick one after another when Jodi asked whether I wanted to take everyone to the Avett Brothers concert in Sioux City. I thought about it for a minute and said sure, but I didn't really mean it. I hadn't been to Sioux City since deciding to close my multistate counseling practice. It was also so hot, and well, I didn't know how I'd feel hearing that music again, and so it felt like a gamble.

So I was reluctant. But I was willing to try and see.

As we loaded the kids into the car and began the hour-long drive, I was thinking about ten different things, and nine and a half of them were negative. When we arrived, we struggled to find parking and then navigated the crowded streets to find a grassy area to sit on among hundreds of other families. A couple of guys were smoking cigarettes and a few couples swayed to the music of the opening acts.

We sat down and listened to an opening act sing some songs about love, and one about swear words, and some about other things that aren't the greatest to highlight in a park full of families with young kids. But overall, the atmosphere was like a family Christmas in July. We were like kids with giant snow cones in hand, in the scorching heat, waiting to see the Avett Brothers.

During the break before the band came out, our kids asked me to take them down to stand in front of the stage, and I did my best to say no while trying to come up with suitable reasons: "I have a cramp" (I didn't), "You'd hate it" (they wouldn't), and my usual ironclad one, "Your mother doesn't want us to" (but she actually did). Like any self-respecting father, I held my ground for a good three minutes, and then agreed and walked them down.

I was the picture of reluctance. But something in me was also willing to be convinced.

We walked the snaking path through the sea of people to an area just in front of the massive stage. I held Finn's and Isla's hands, and Ollie bounced along right behind. We came to a spot directly in front of the stage, right next to a couple who were laughing as they shared a vape pen, and a woman who was far more excited to be standing there than I was. When the music started, I hoisted Finn up to sit on my shoulders, and a song or two into things, the kids started dancing, and I sort of did too, mostly to blend in and for Finn's sake. It was hard not to dance standing there as the sun set and everyone else swayed around us. I tried not to think about that song and sent up a quick half-hearted prayer that they might just skip it or forget to play it, and I'd be okay. Maybe this wouldn't have to be like that night in Chicago all over again and I could just move on.

But we all know that's not how it works.

The band started playing the chords of "I and Love and You" not long after. Finn's feet hung in my face, sweat beaded on my forehead, and my chest started to tighten up. The kids had no idea what this song meant to us, the thousand-pound weight that was attached to it, and I was glad for them.

I stared at the ground for what felt like eternity, and when I looked up, suddenly Jodi was standing there looking at me. She had made her way down to us when she heard the song start. The look on her face said everything; all the words I'd been trying not to say or even think were suddenly the only things I could think of. All of it was unspoken, but we were both thinking we had come a long way from that day of the longest drive when everything had felt so hopeless.

Against the longest odds, the science, and the grief we'd carried, we now had three beautiful kids, and here they all were in front of a stage at a concert in this beautiful setting as the light in the sky dimmed and faded. It wasn't perfection, and plenty in our life was still difficult, but that all was far away now. Tears welled up in my eyes, but these were different emotions. Amid these people I loved and was connected to, it was a different experience. The song had become a bookmark now in the pages of my life rather than a bookend. The journey here had been anything but easy, but we'd kept going, and everything looked different, fuller somehow. It was no longer about whether we would have kids or what I'd been through but instead about our working through it together. Some things from that day had never gotten better, but in this moment I realized that wasn't the point.

I'd learned from a wise colleague that when I wanted to remind myself to receive what's happening in the moment, I could open my hands as a physical expression of it. As the tears fell down my cheeks, I did it: I opened my hands. It dawned on me that this whole time I had been looking at my experiences and listening to this song like it was an anchor tied to my ankle, it was actually a springboard to something better. To get through it and come out on the other side, I had needed to shift from seeing only what I was missing to the possibility of what I might receive. And although it looked the same, it was different because I saw that there were people around me who loved me. I wasn't alone and didn't have to be. Connection was possible, and I had always been loved even in those moments when I was sure I wasn't.

This story isn't about everything working out, because that's not true. It doesn't always. Sometimes we experience loss and pain that simply stop us in our tracks and never get redeemed. There's nothing to say there, no silver lining, and it doesn't work out the way we think it should for everyone. And yet we get to decide what we do with that, because that part is in our control. And the question is, Do we hold on to those experiences tightly, refusing to let go, or do we move on? It's up to us. It's always up to us.

What our world needs now more than ever is people who are willing to face and move beyond their past to pursue what God calls them to. Making this effort changes not only your life but the legacy of your family, the trajectory of your relationships, and the world in general. It is hard work, but it will always be worth it.

You might ask yourself why change should start with you, but I'd ask, Why not you?

The version of me sitting in that apartment twenty years ago never would have guessed that he'd end up here today. He just wouldn't have. He was full of stories that he was either too unique or not unique enough, that people wouldn't care, and that he couldn't do it alone. And he was partially right. He wasn't that unique, and he couldn't do it alone. But it was never about that. Instead, it was about opening his hands and his heart and taking the next step.

Take sixty seconds to hold your hands out in front of you and open them up. Are they empty? Or are they open?

ACKNOWLEDGMENTS

Writing this first book felt a bit like moving into a new home. It was a huge project, and although I'm the one who gets to live in the new house, I know that I didn't get here alone and that the freezer didn't move itself.

Jodi, thank you for all your encouragement and support. You have been an editor, listener, problem solver, and partner this entire time. J. Oliver, Isla, and Finn, thank you for encouraging me to pursue this dream and making it fun along the way.

Kaylyn Mehlhaff, your editing and guidance have played an instrumental role in this project. Mick Silva, thanks for helping me talk through the ideas and being a sounding board and editor.

Mike Vaughn, your friendship and encouragement have been life giving. Tony Boer, thank you for being a fixture in my life. I couldn't begin to express my gratitude here. Adam Weber, thank you for driving me forward and believing in this project even when I didn't. I wouldn't have had this book without you. Mary Bellofatto, you are an expert, a loyal friend, a mentor, and an integral part of my breakthrough. To my friends and family at Bethesda Workshops, thank you for your support and for eating lots of Jeni's ice cream with me along the way.

Huge thank you to Tom Dean for giving me this opportunity and being a wonderful guide and advocate. To the team at Zondervan, thank you for your support, guidance, and encouragement.

Family, friends, and relatives, thank you for your encouragement. To my clients, you have taught me just as much as I could teach you. It is an honor to be a part of your story and have a voice in your life.

Last but not least, thank you, God. I've been given more grace than I deserve, and it's not lost on me. I hope this book honors others and reflects the love I've been shown.